I0426944

I dedicate this little coloring book for children to God. In this world with so much technology, I hope that our children will disconnect a little from their cell phones and tablets and literally put their hands on colored pencils, brushes, and paint pots.
I thank my beloved wife, mother, and grandmother Angela for her encouragement and support. I love you!

Sergio Lourenço
2024

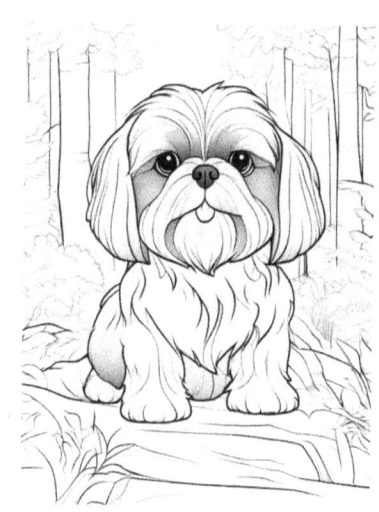

This Book Belongs to:

○───────────────────────────────────────○

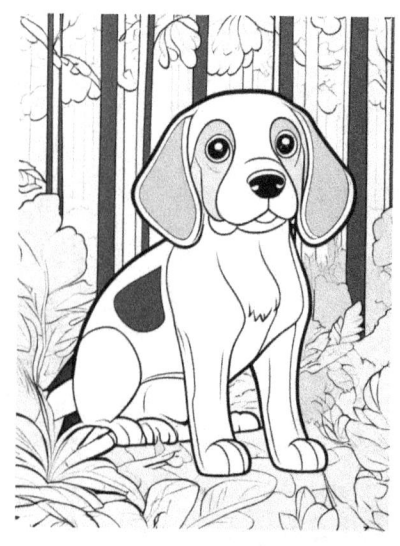

S.L.P.©
all rights reserved

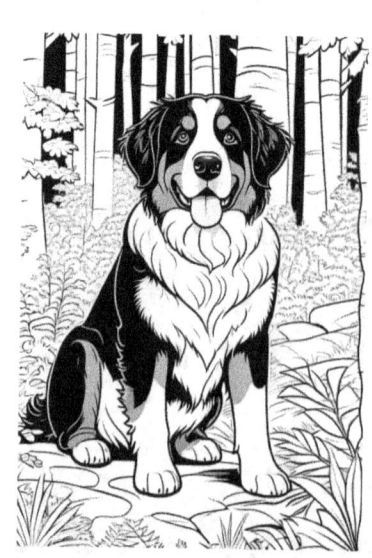

ALL RIGHTS RESERVED ©
2024

No part of this publication may be reproduced, distributed, or transmitted in any form or by any means, including photocopying, recording, or other electronic or mechanical methods, without the prior written permission of the publisher, except for brief quotations incorporated in critical reviews and other specific noncommercial uses. Any unauthorized replica of this work is prohibited.

S.L.P.©
Sergio Lourenço publications

Test Color Page

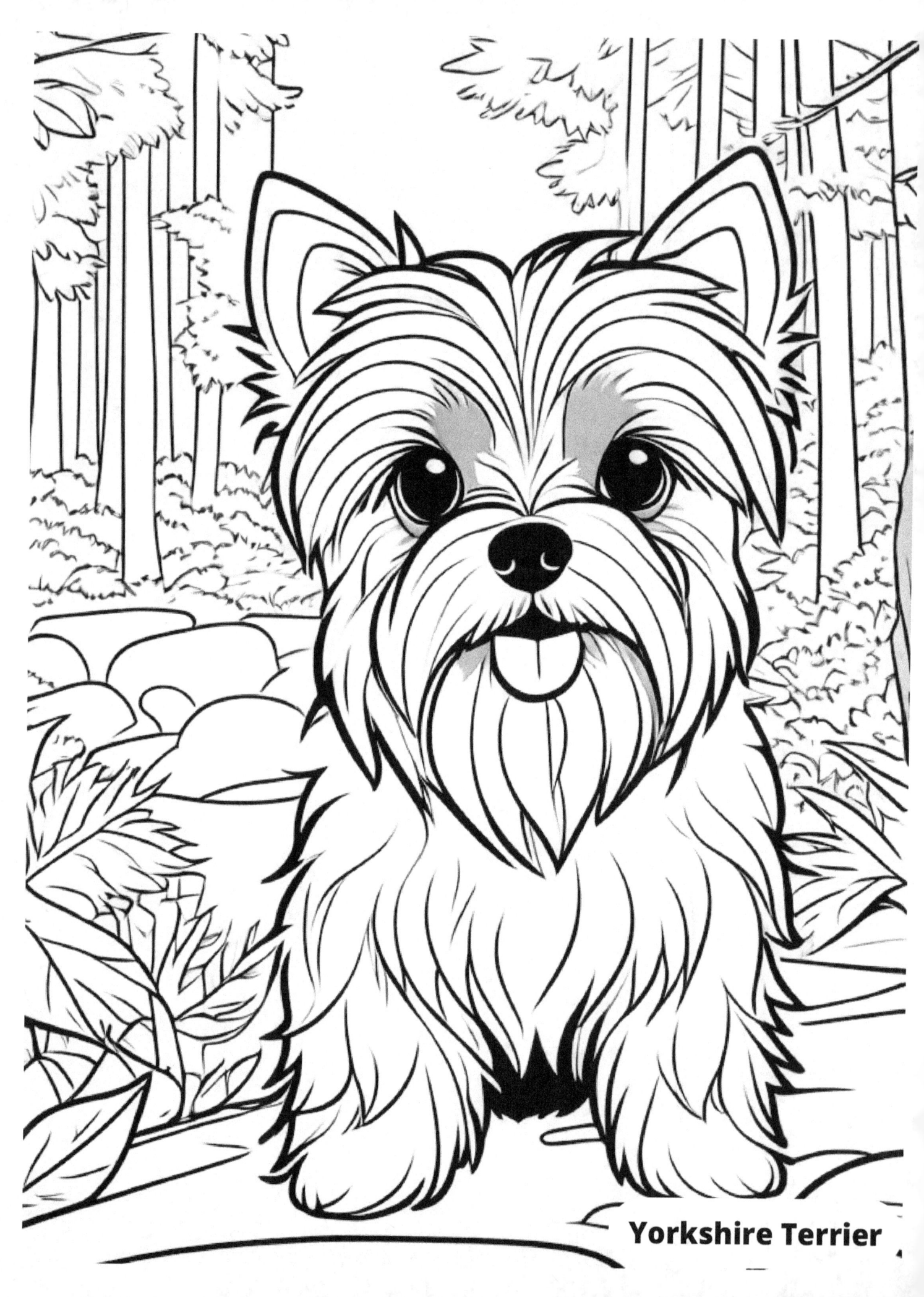

Yorkshire Terrier

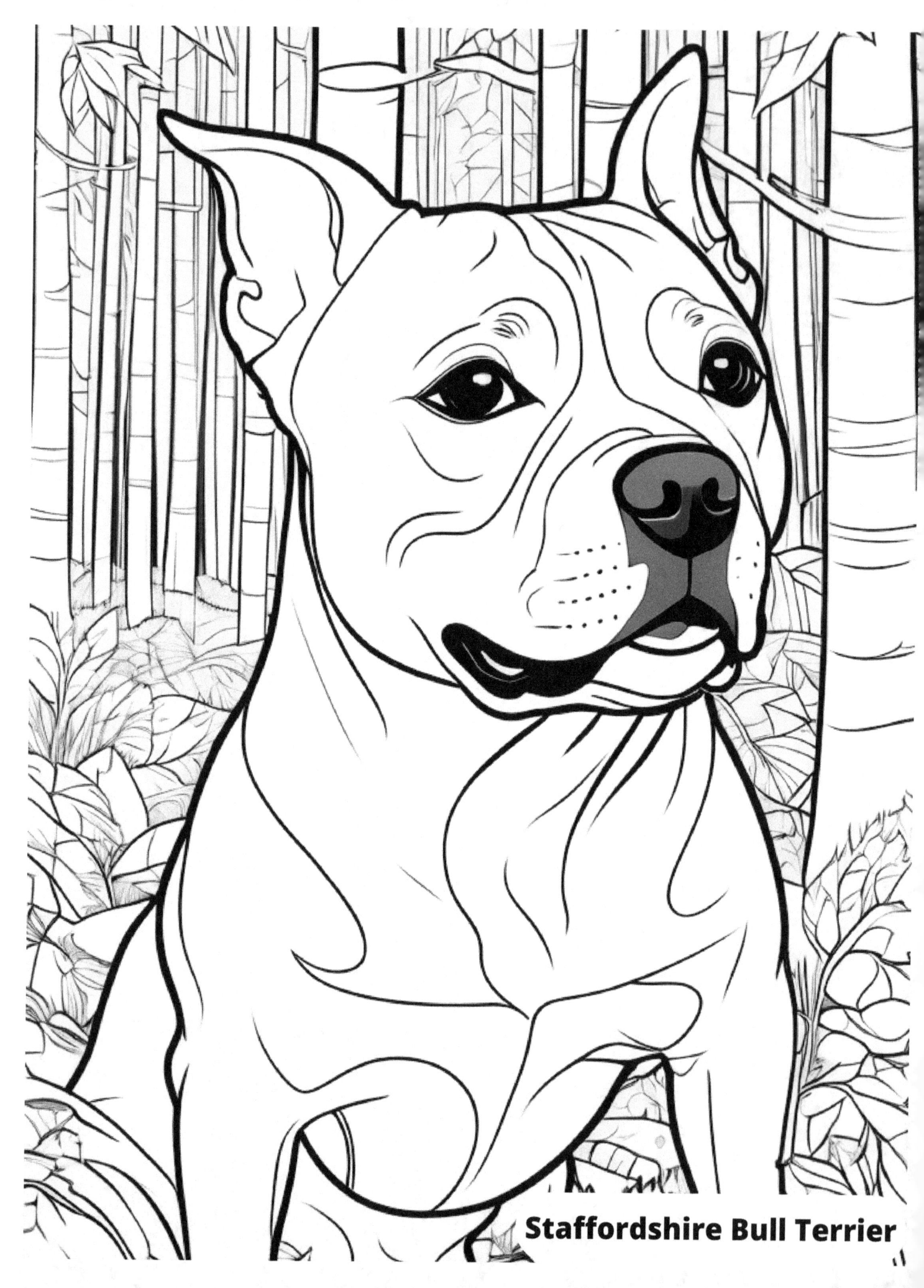

Staffordshire Bull Terrier

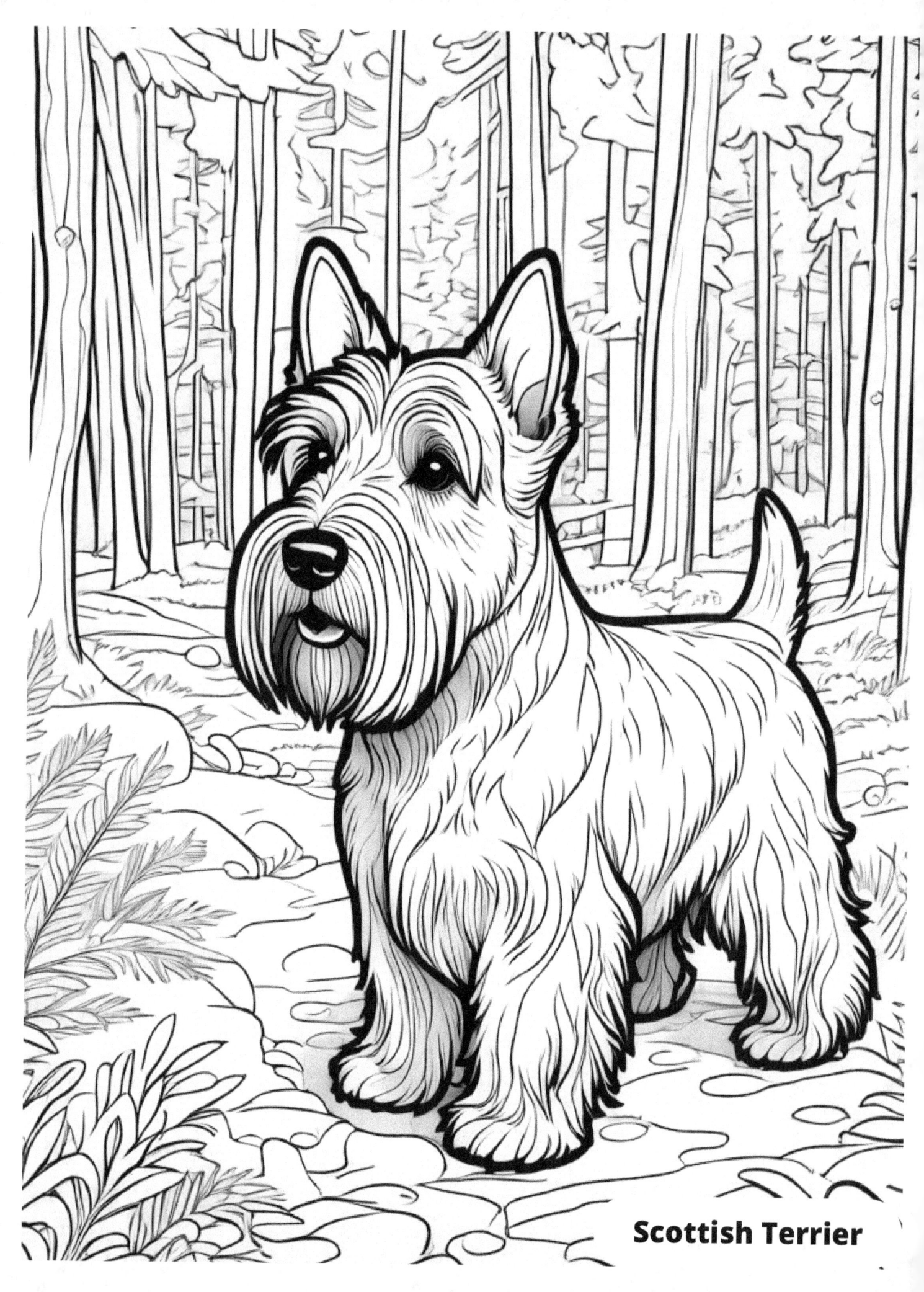

Scottish Terrier

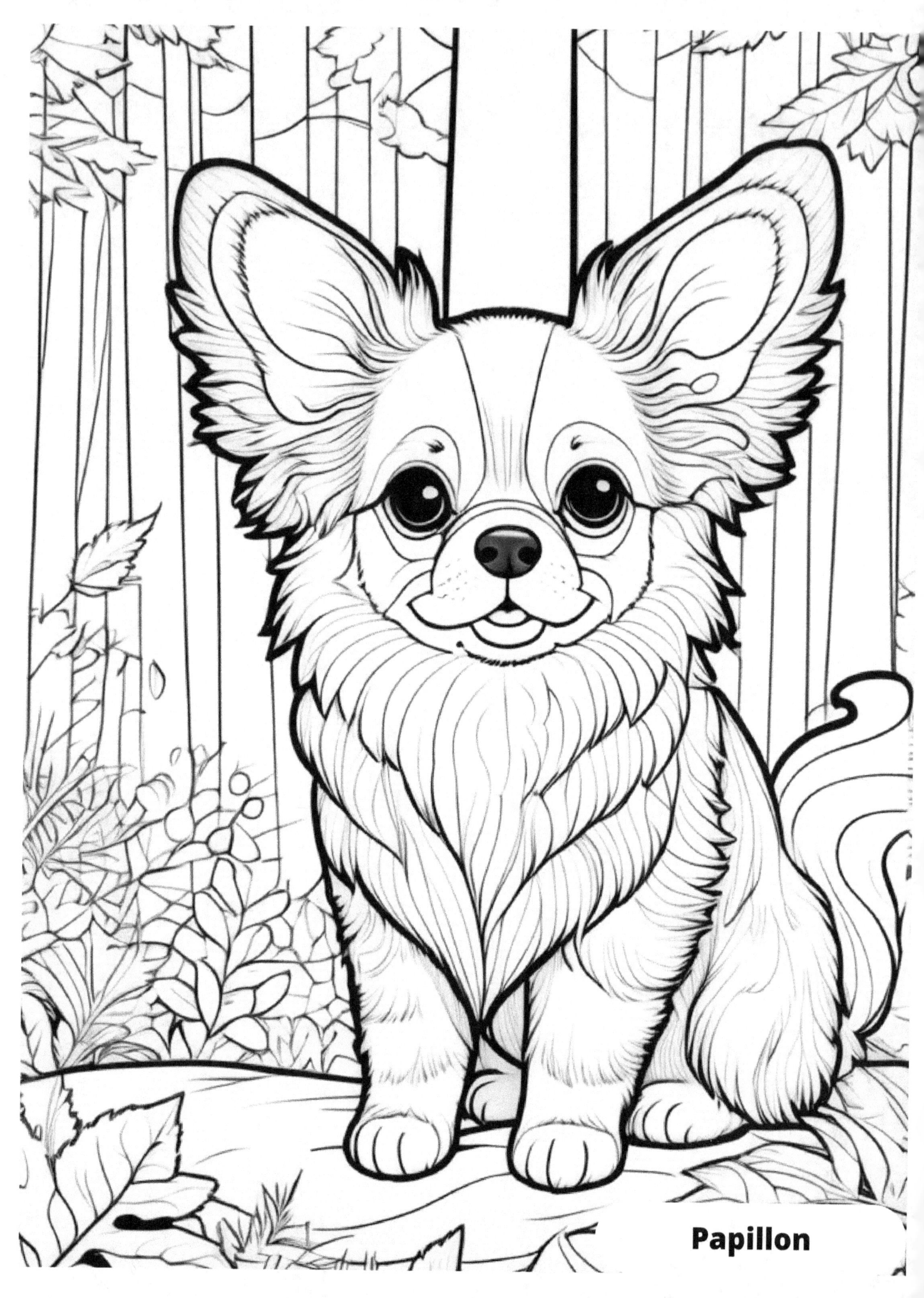

Papillon

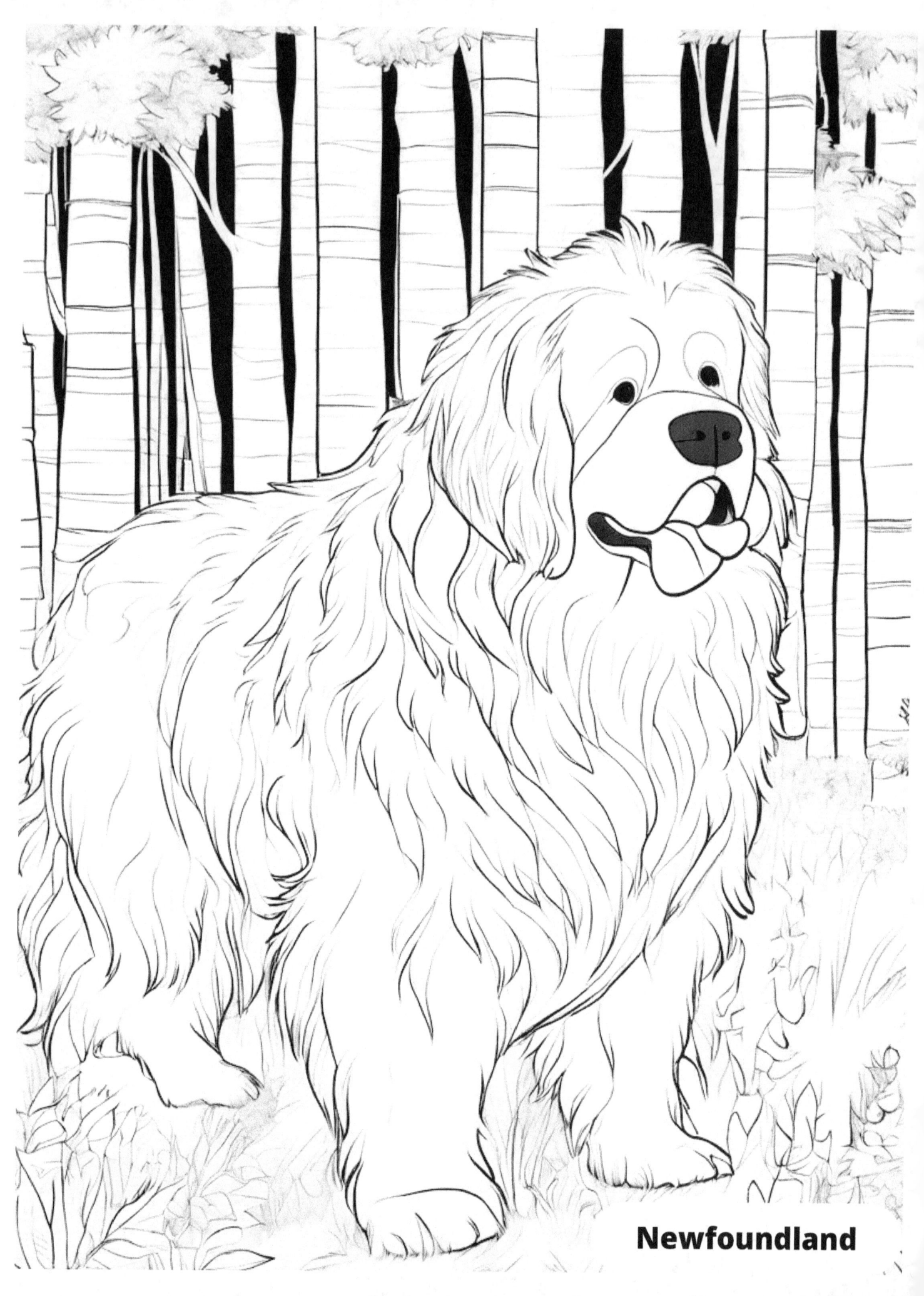

Newfoundland

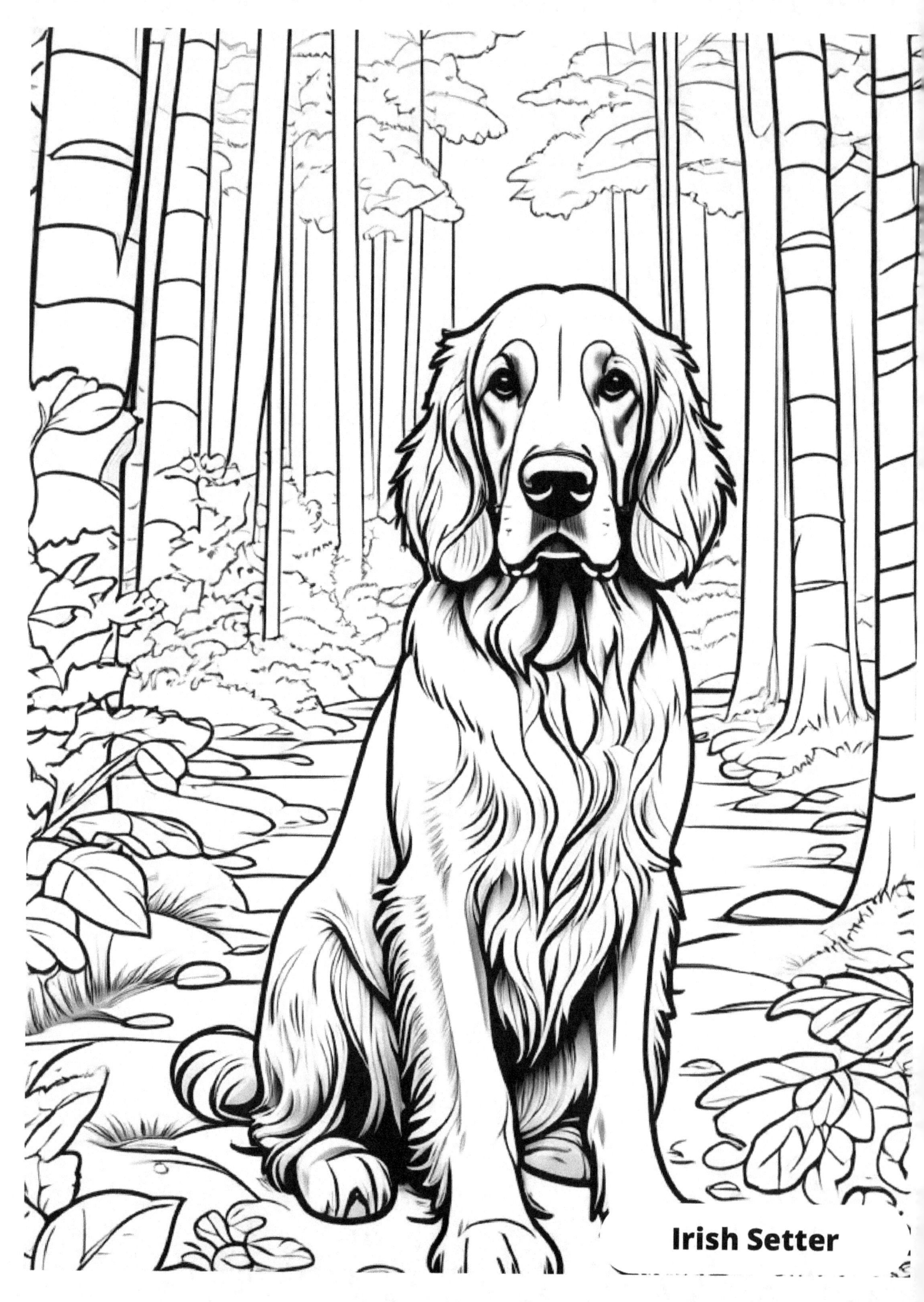

Irish Setter

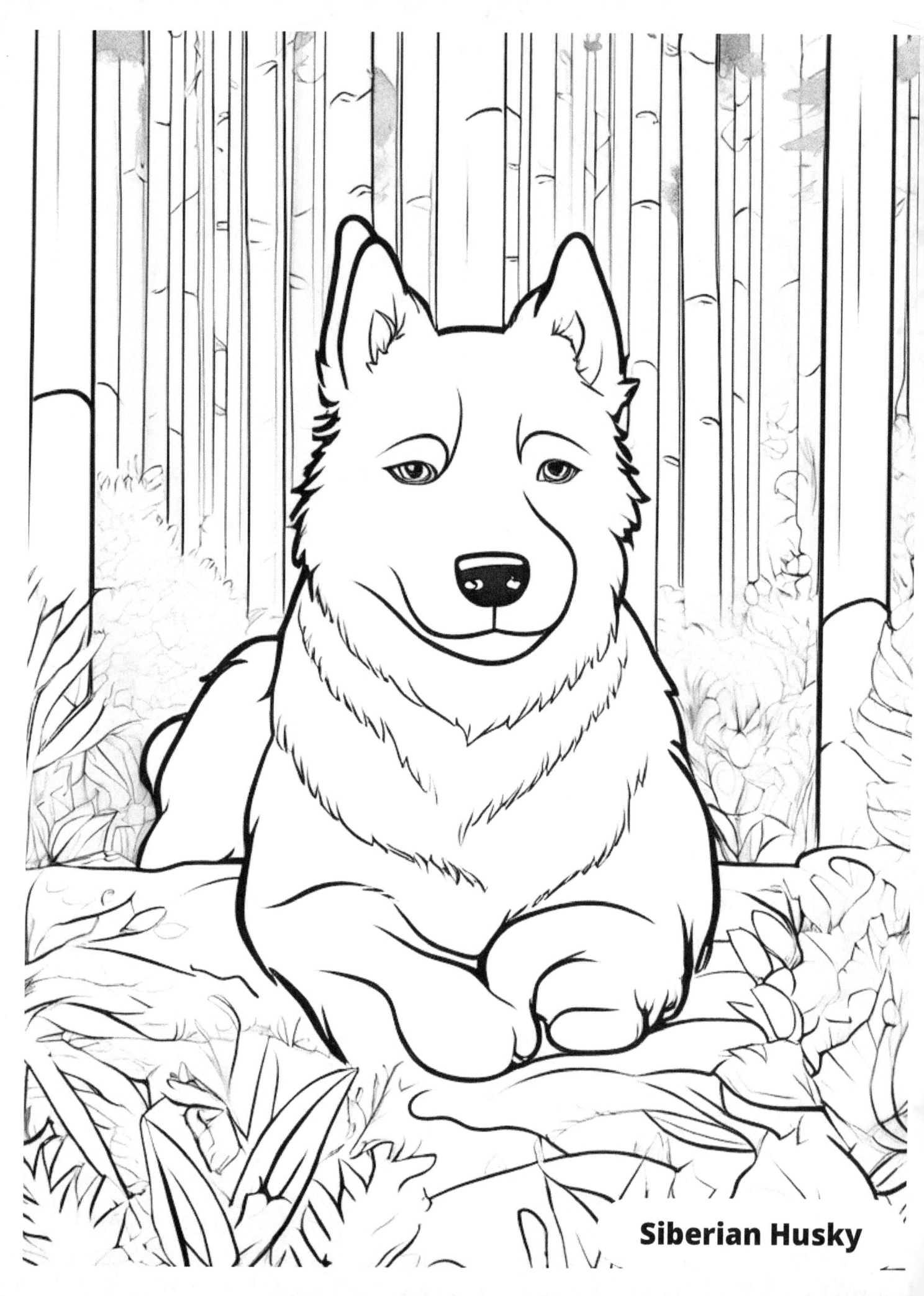

Siberian Husky

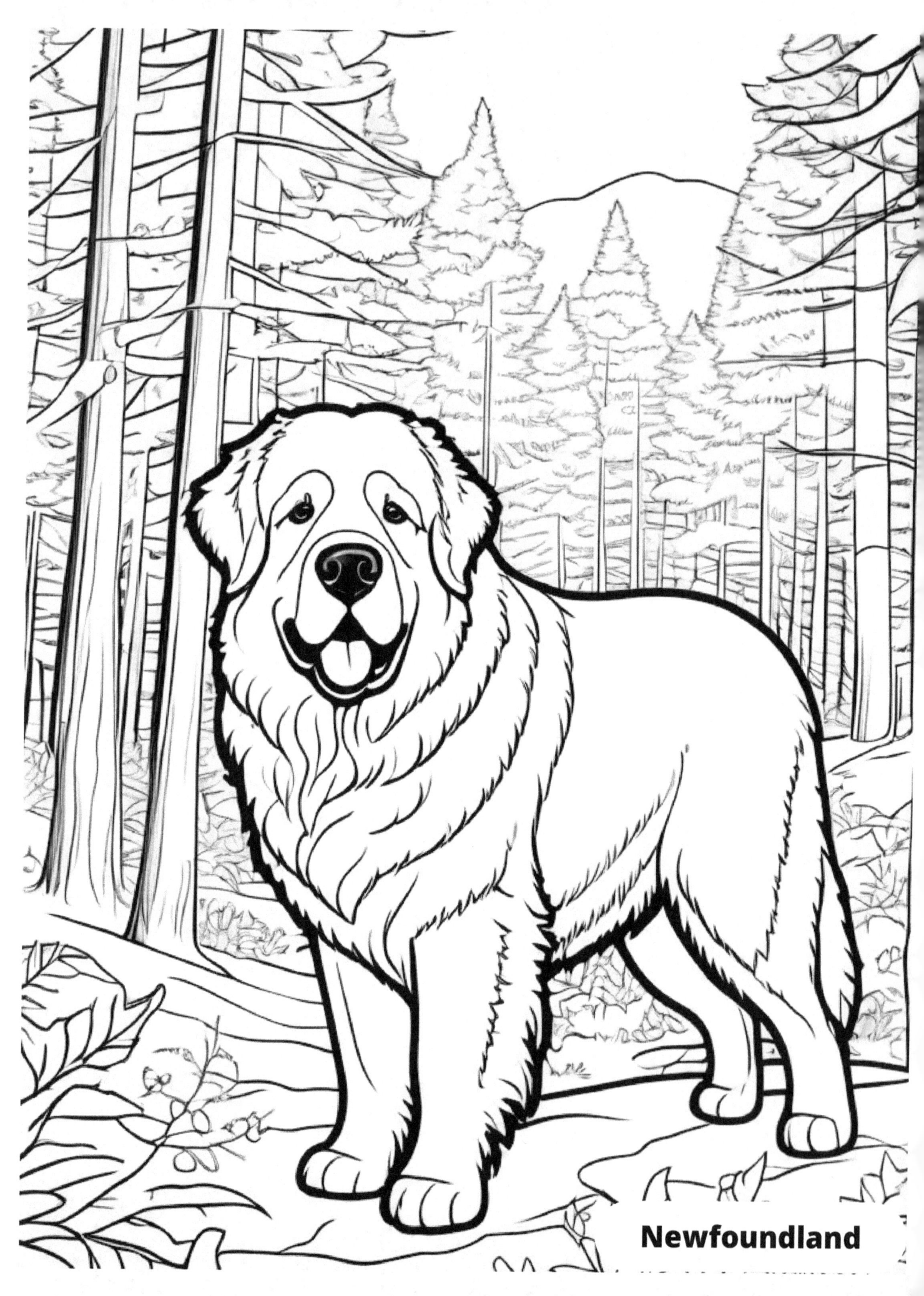

Newfoundland

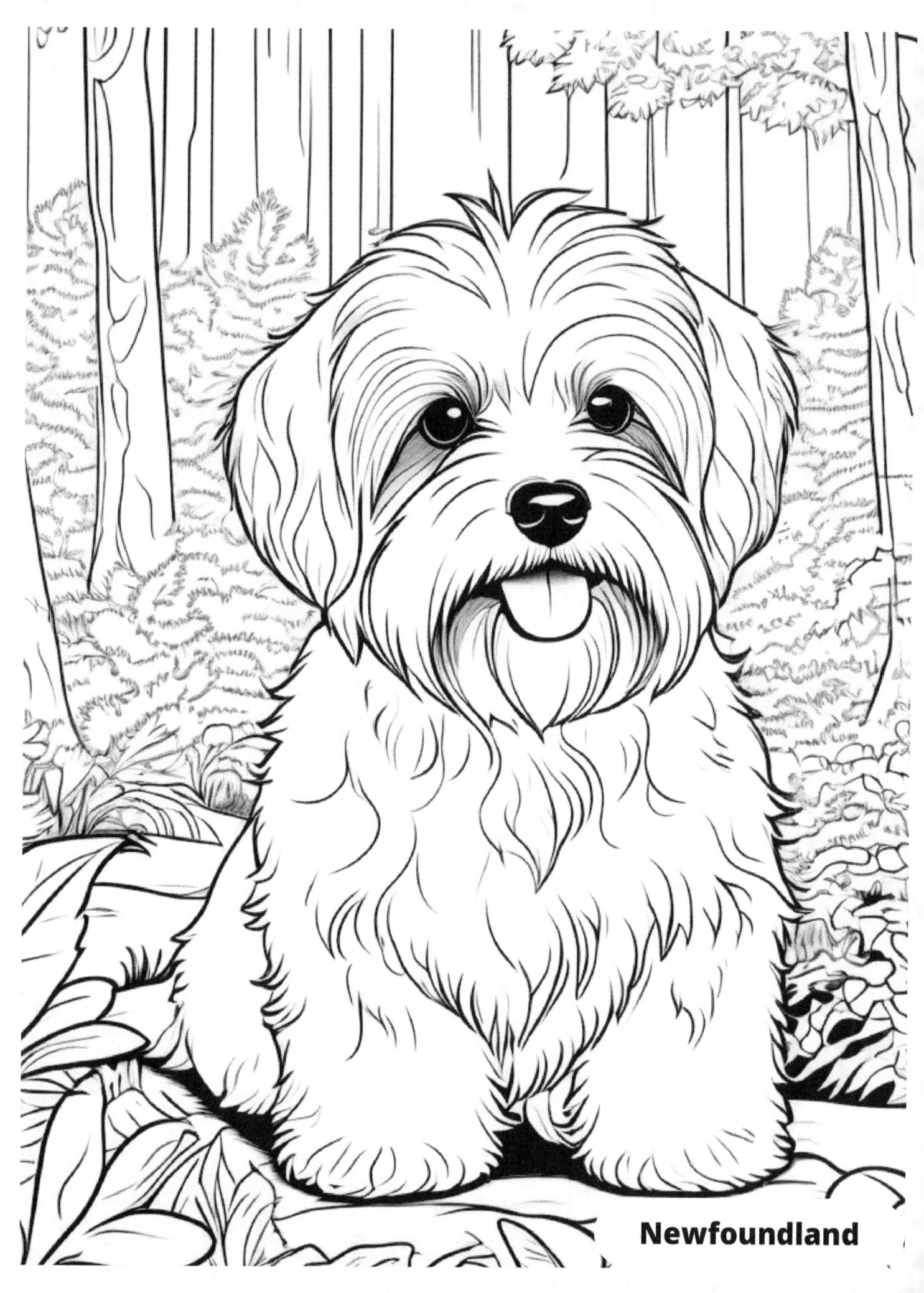

Newfoundland

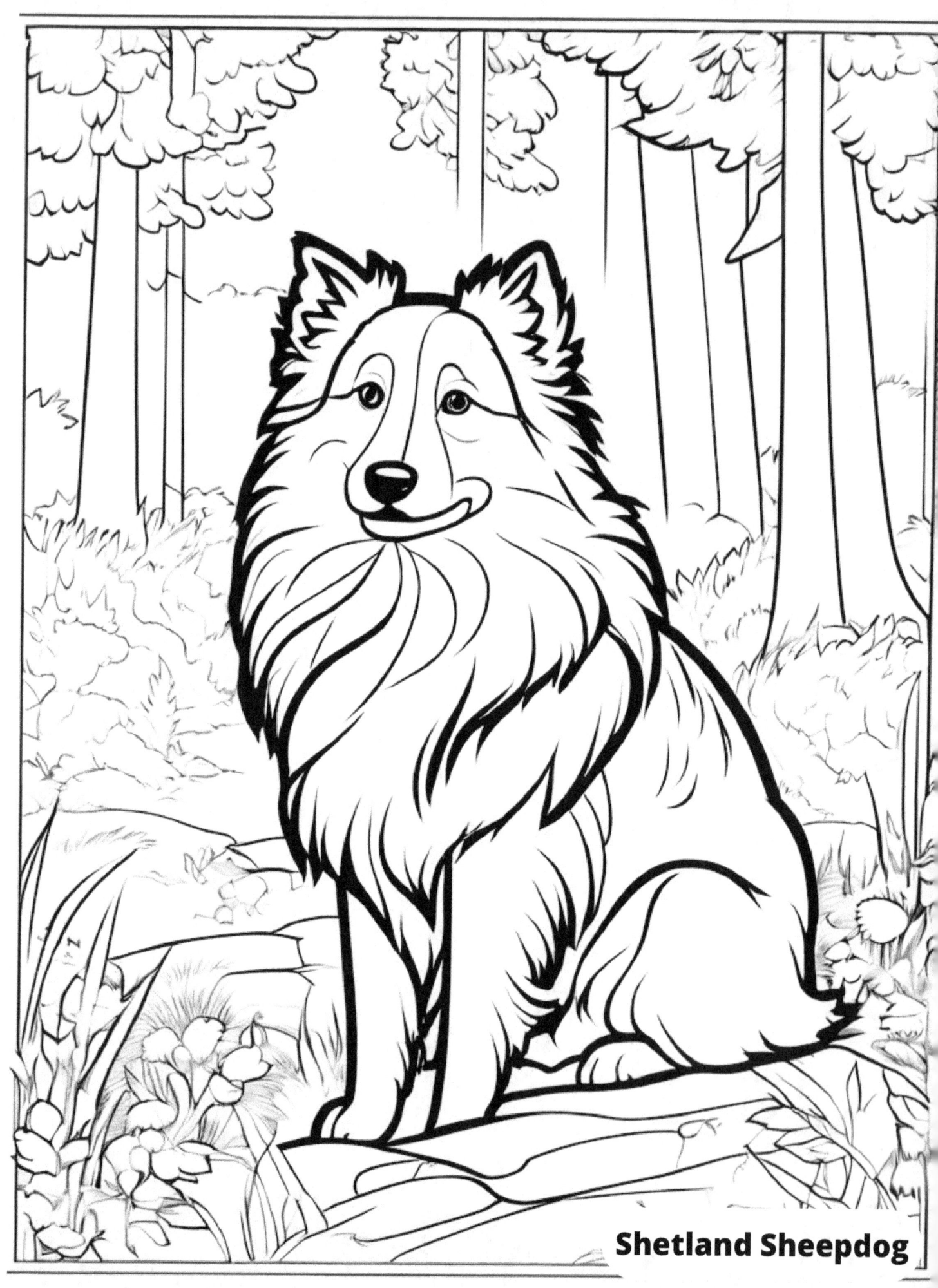

Shetland Sheepdog

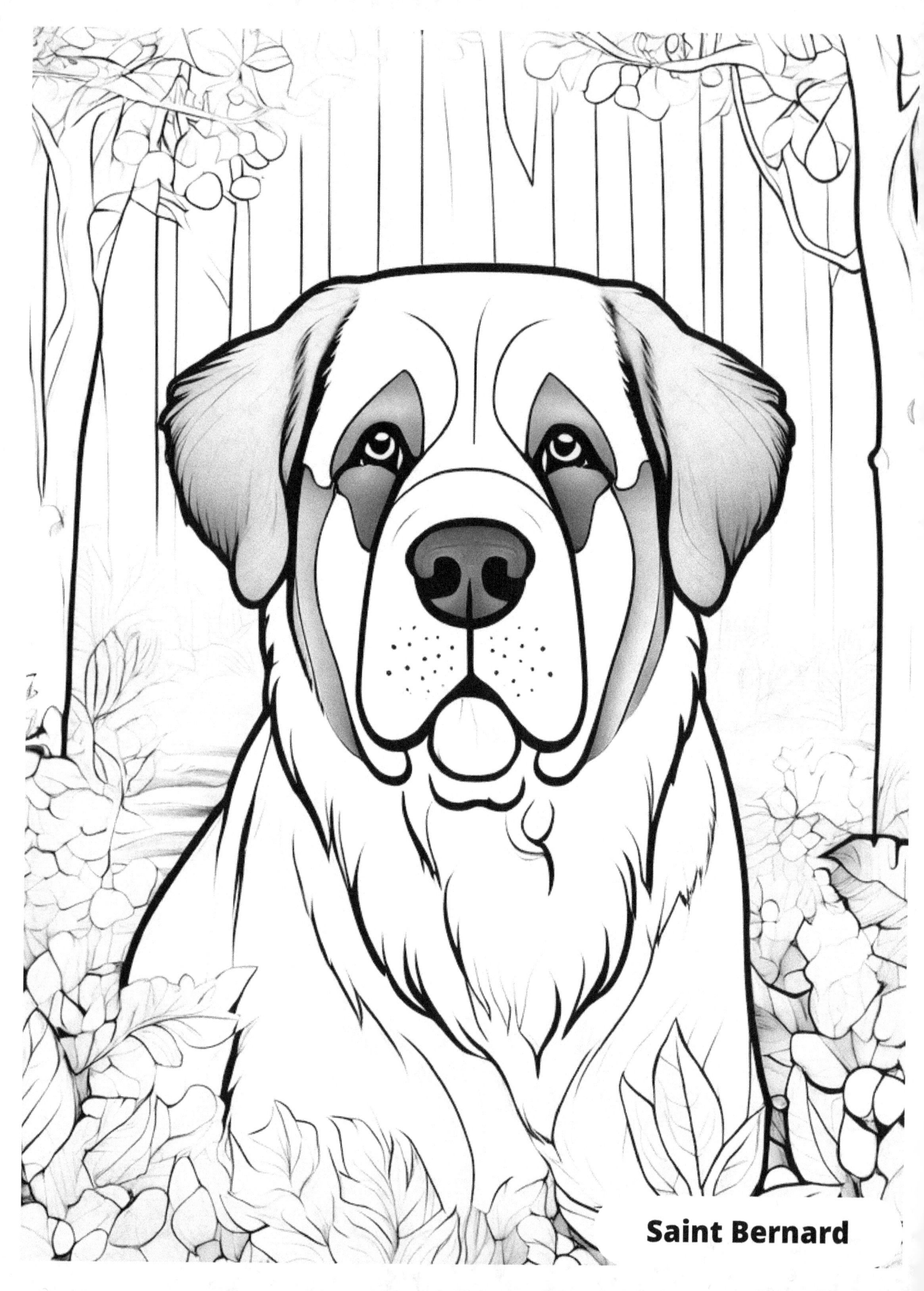

Saint Bernard

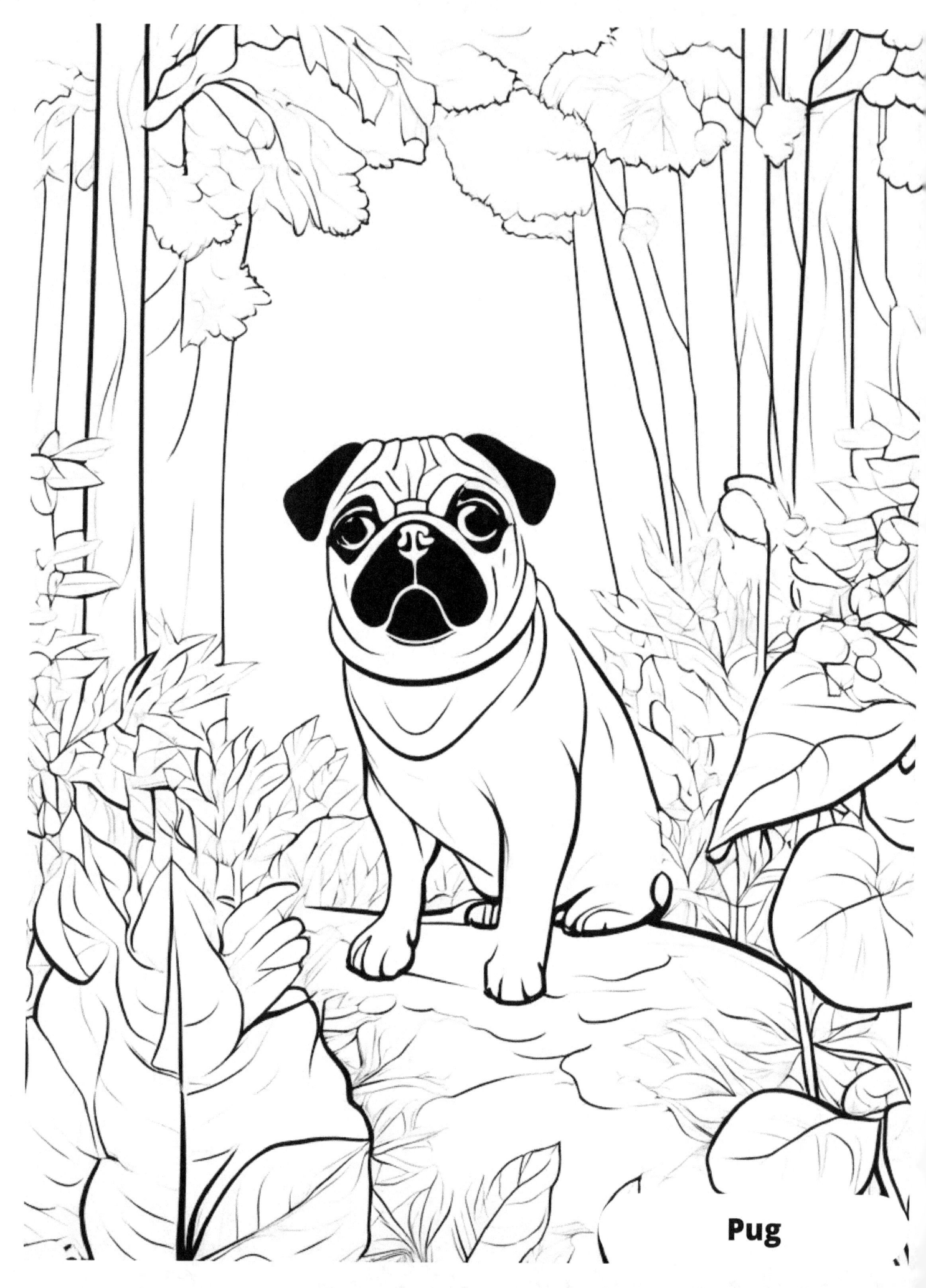

Pug

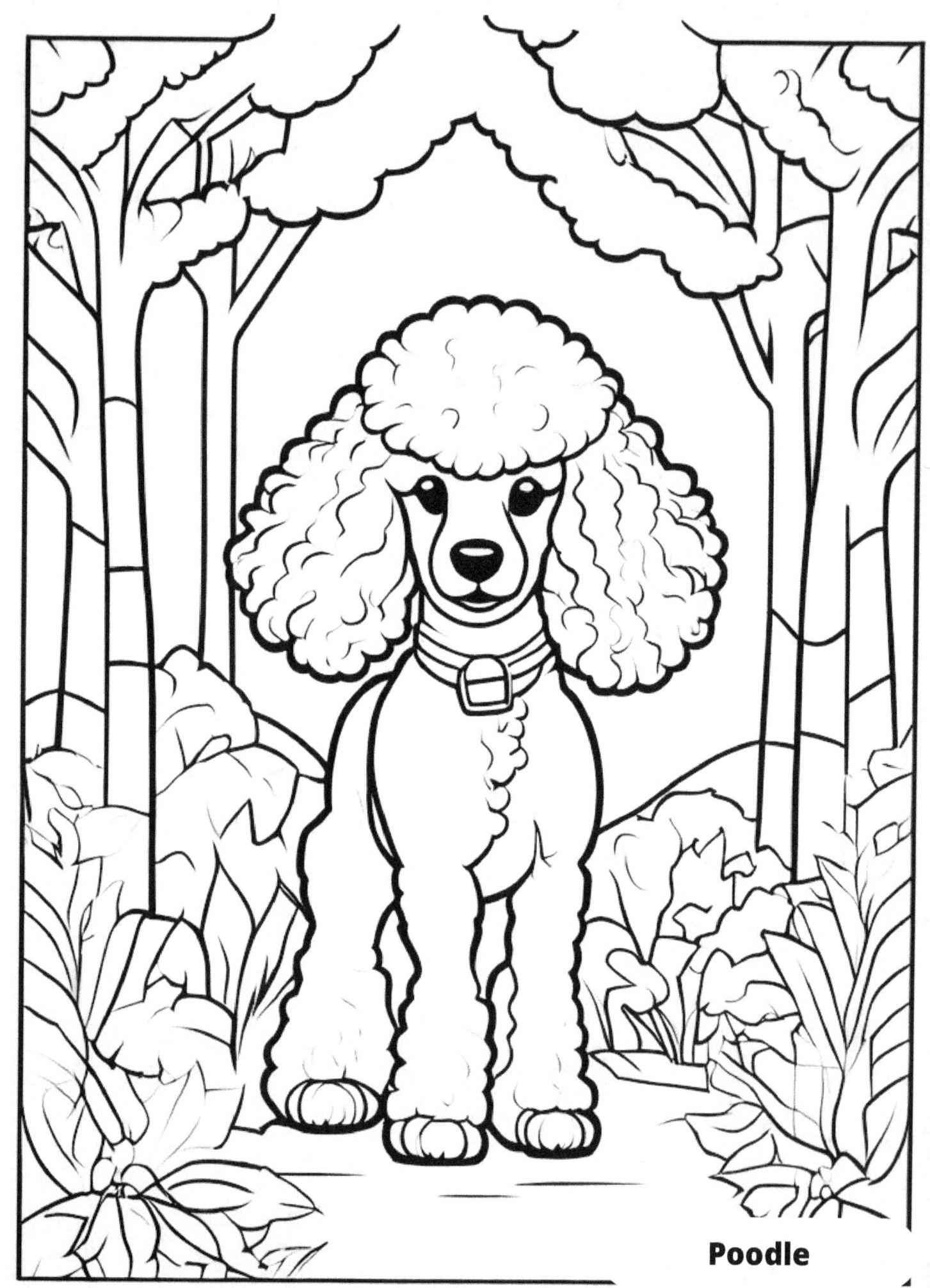

Poodle

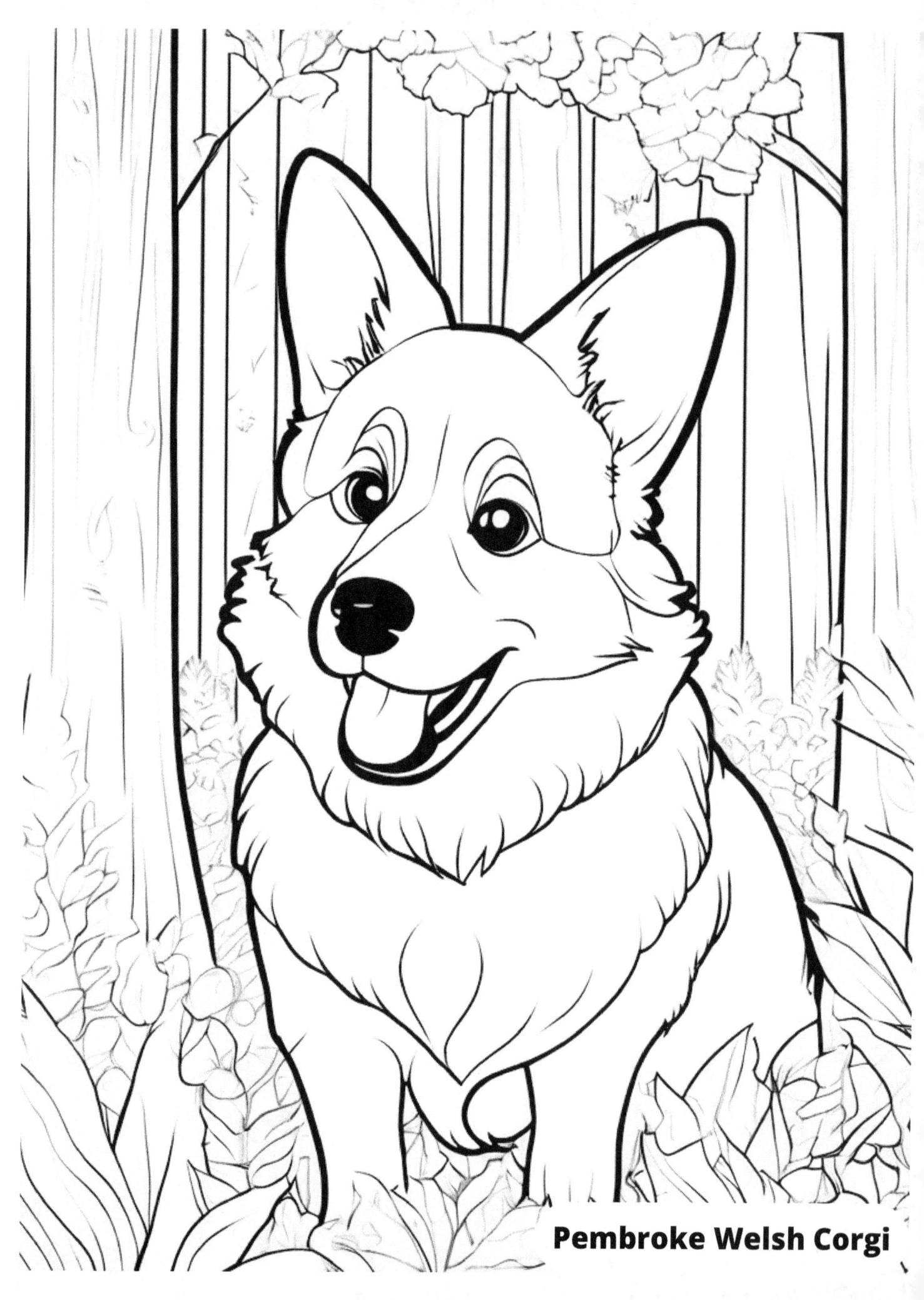

Pembroke Welsh Corgi

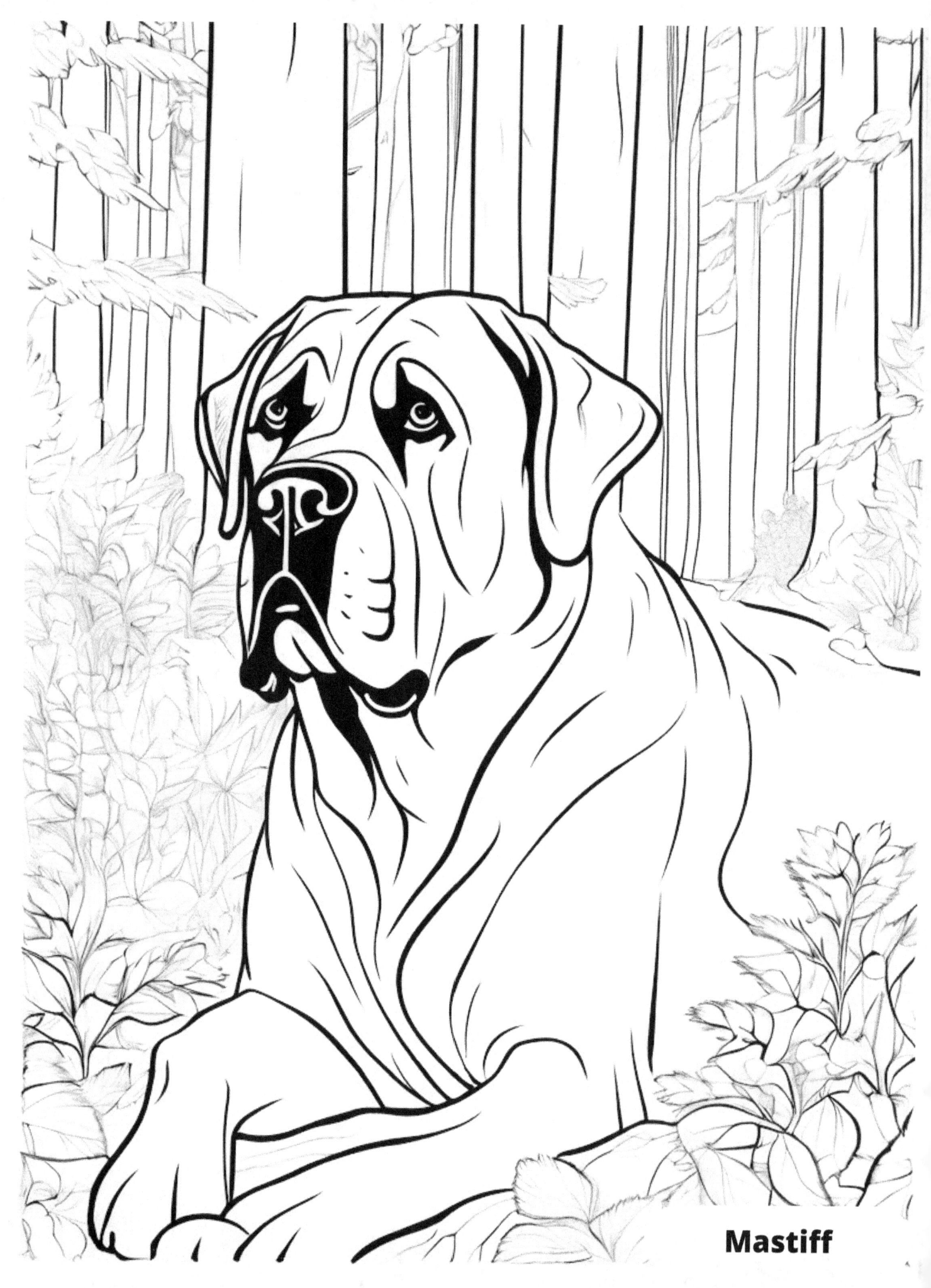

Mastiff

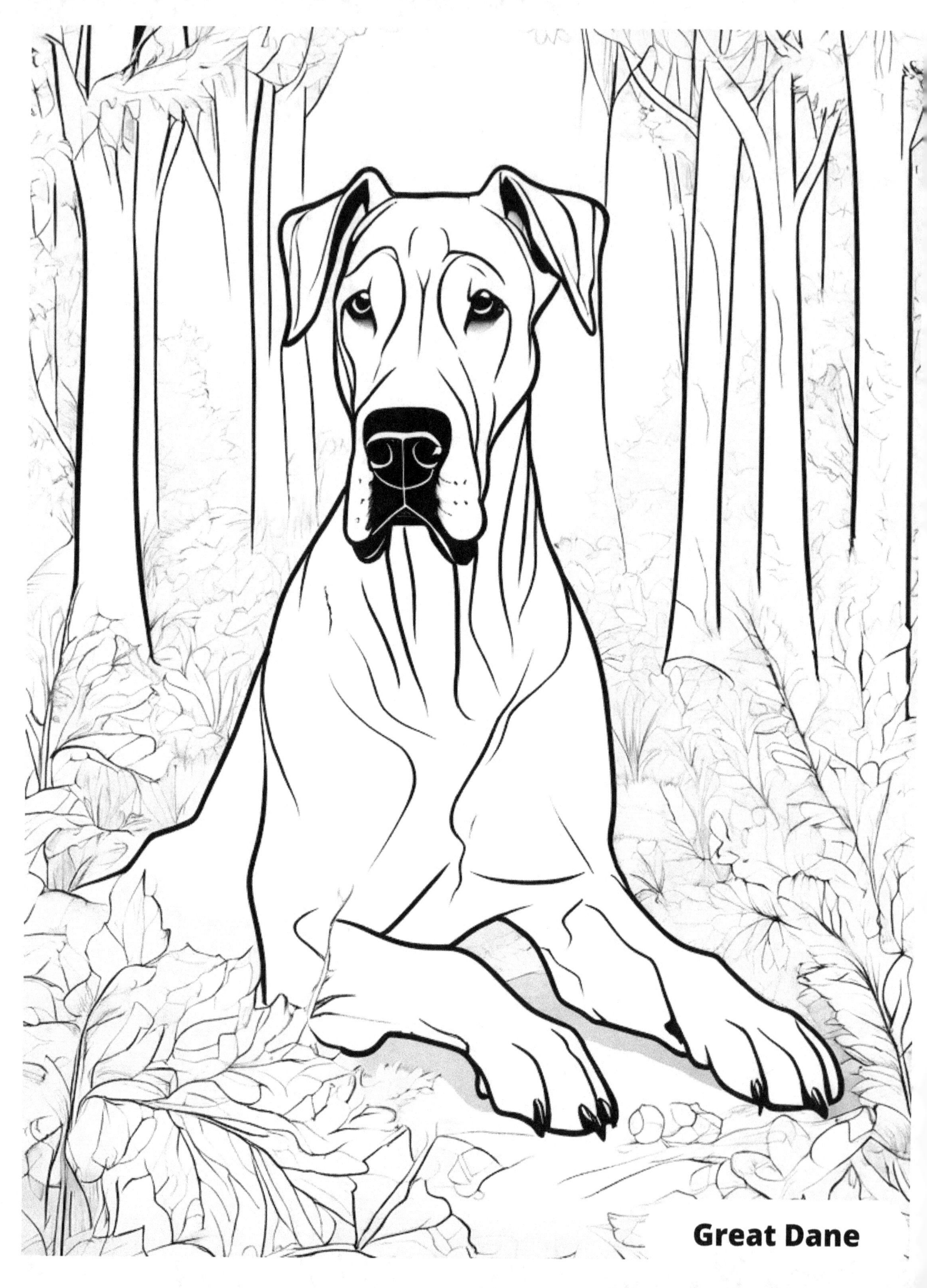

Great Dane

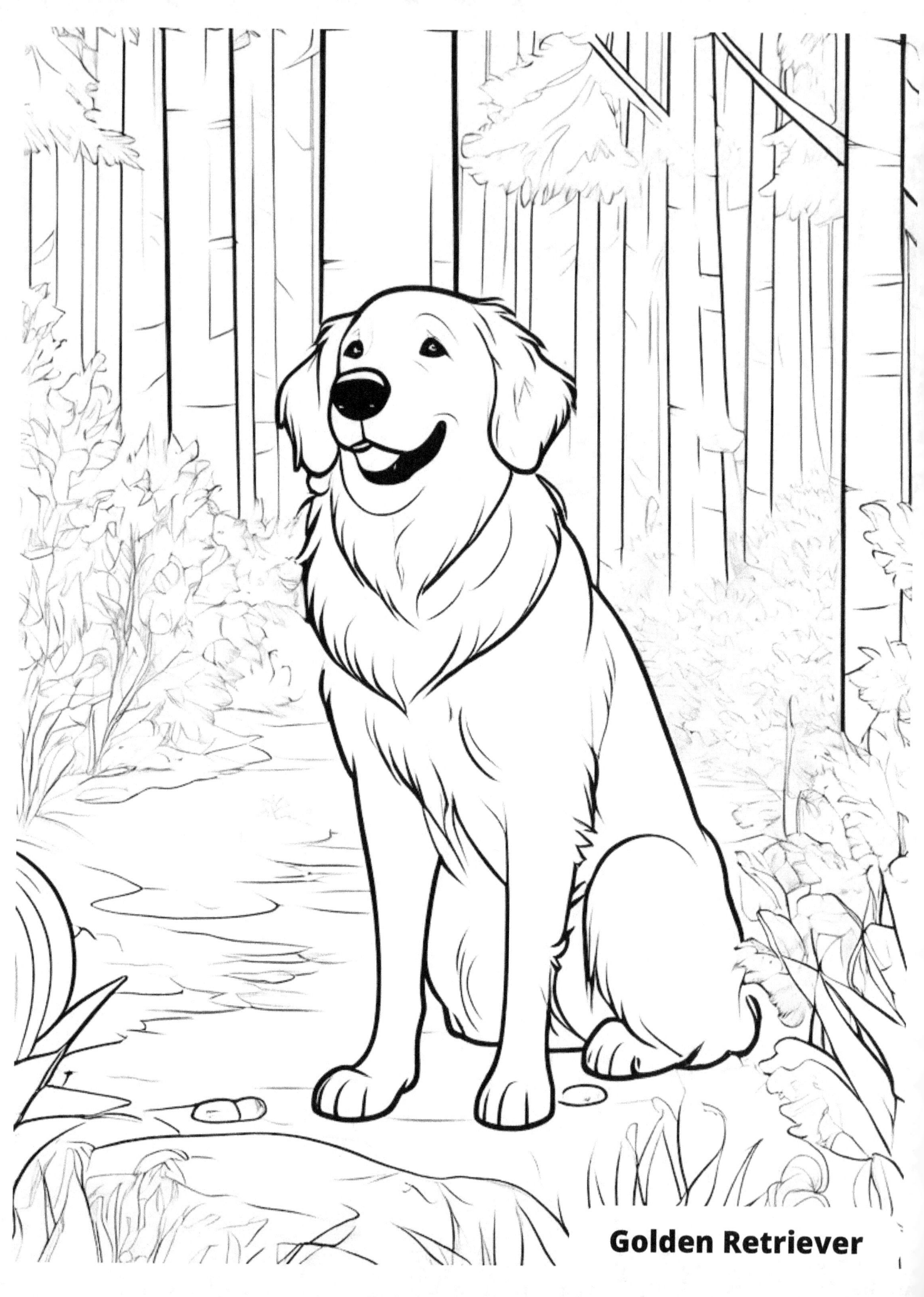

Golden Retriever

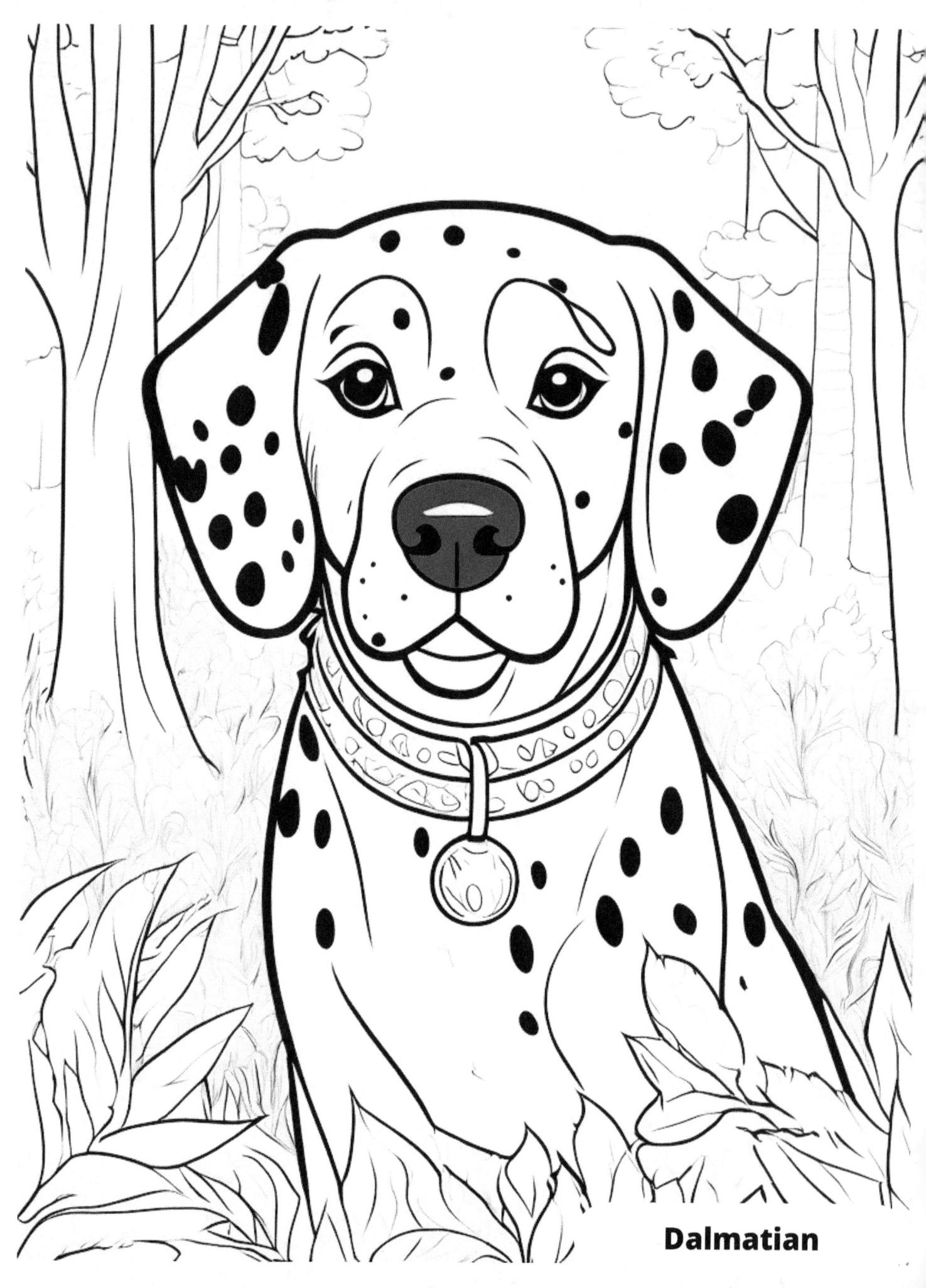

Dalmatian

D. Takahashi

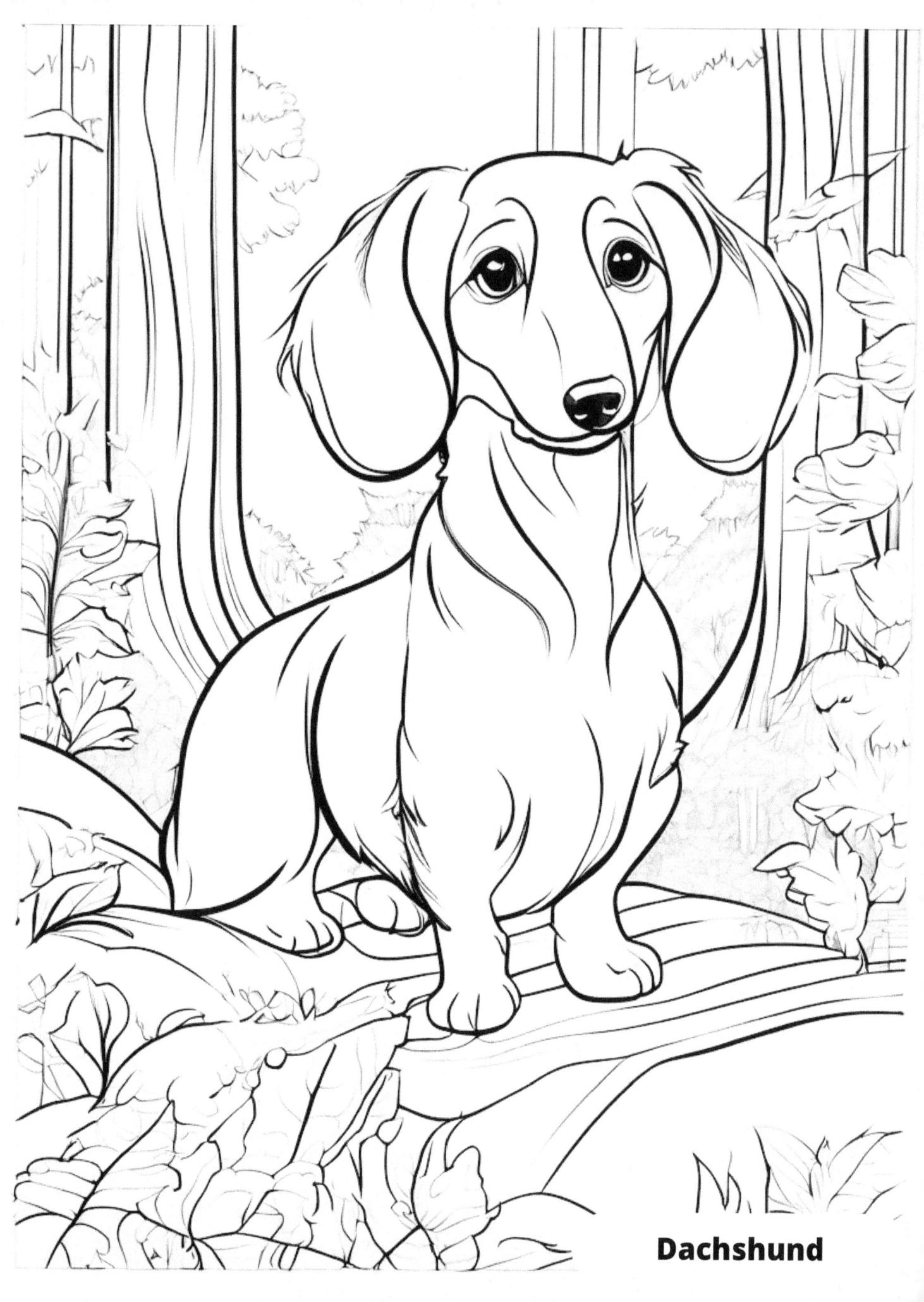

Dachshund

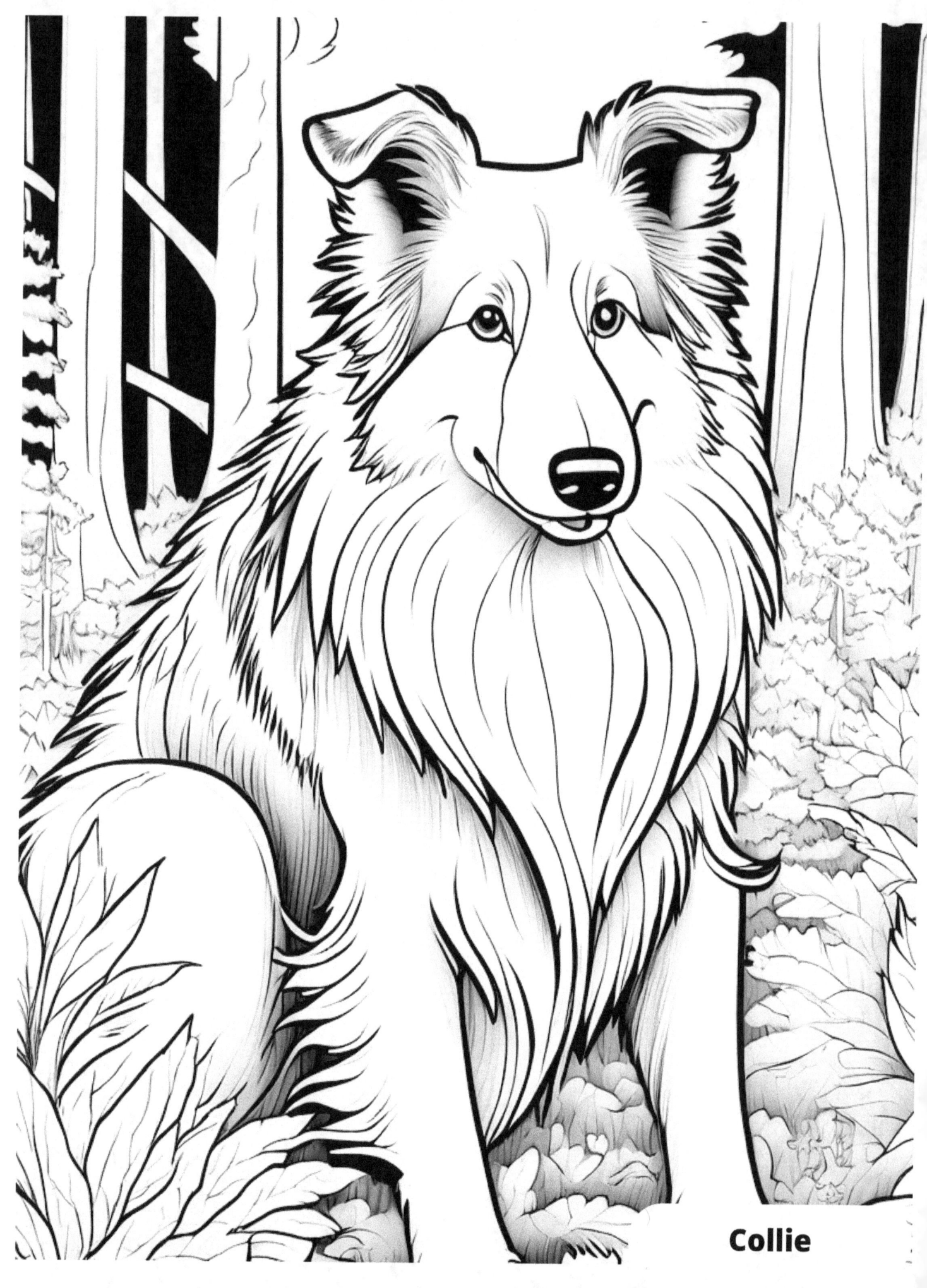

Collie

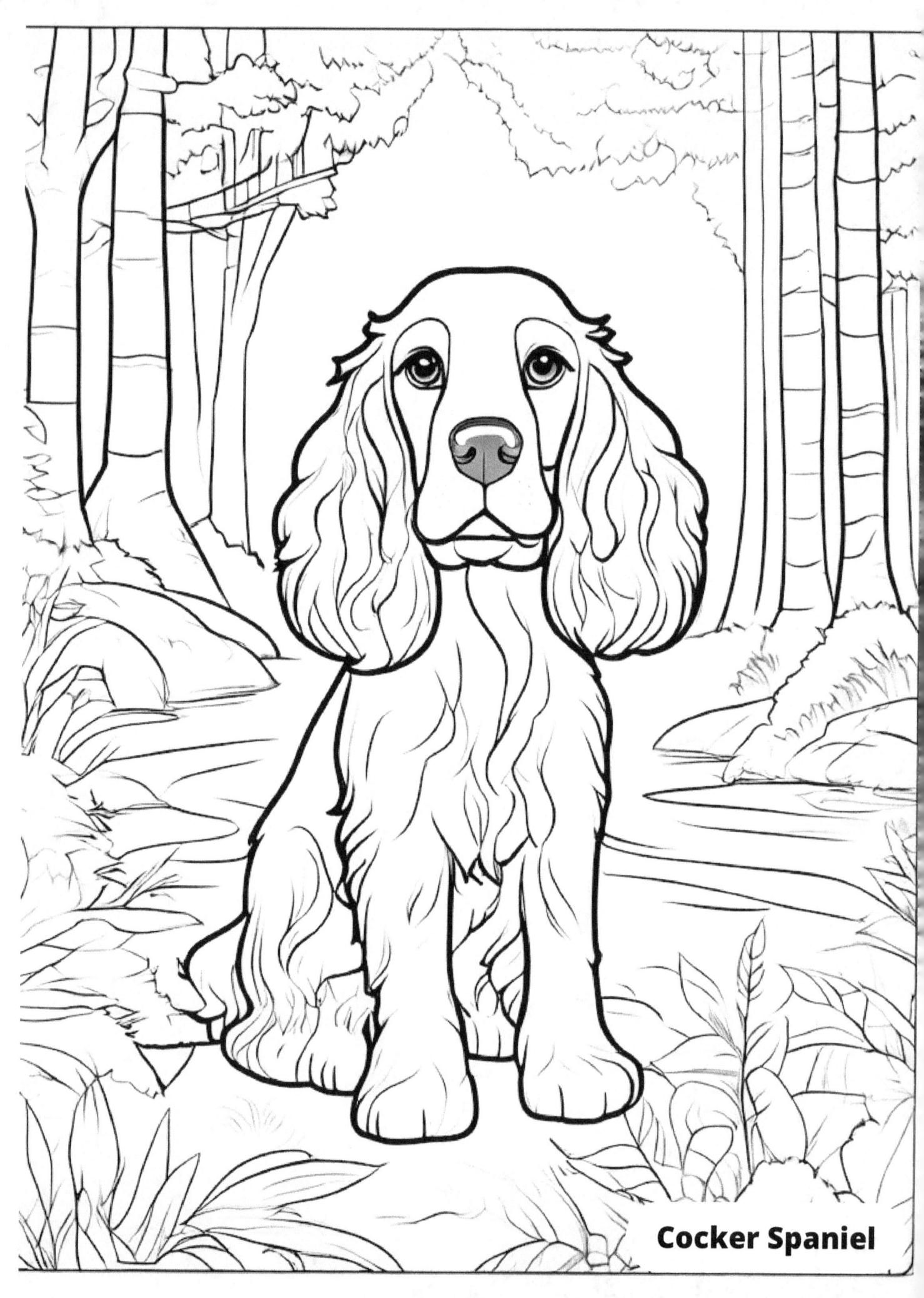

Cocker Spaniel

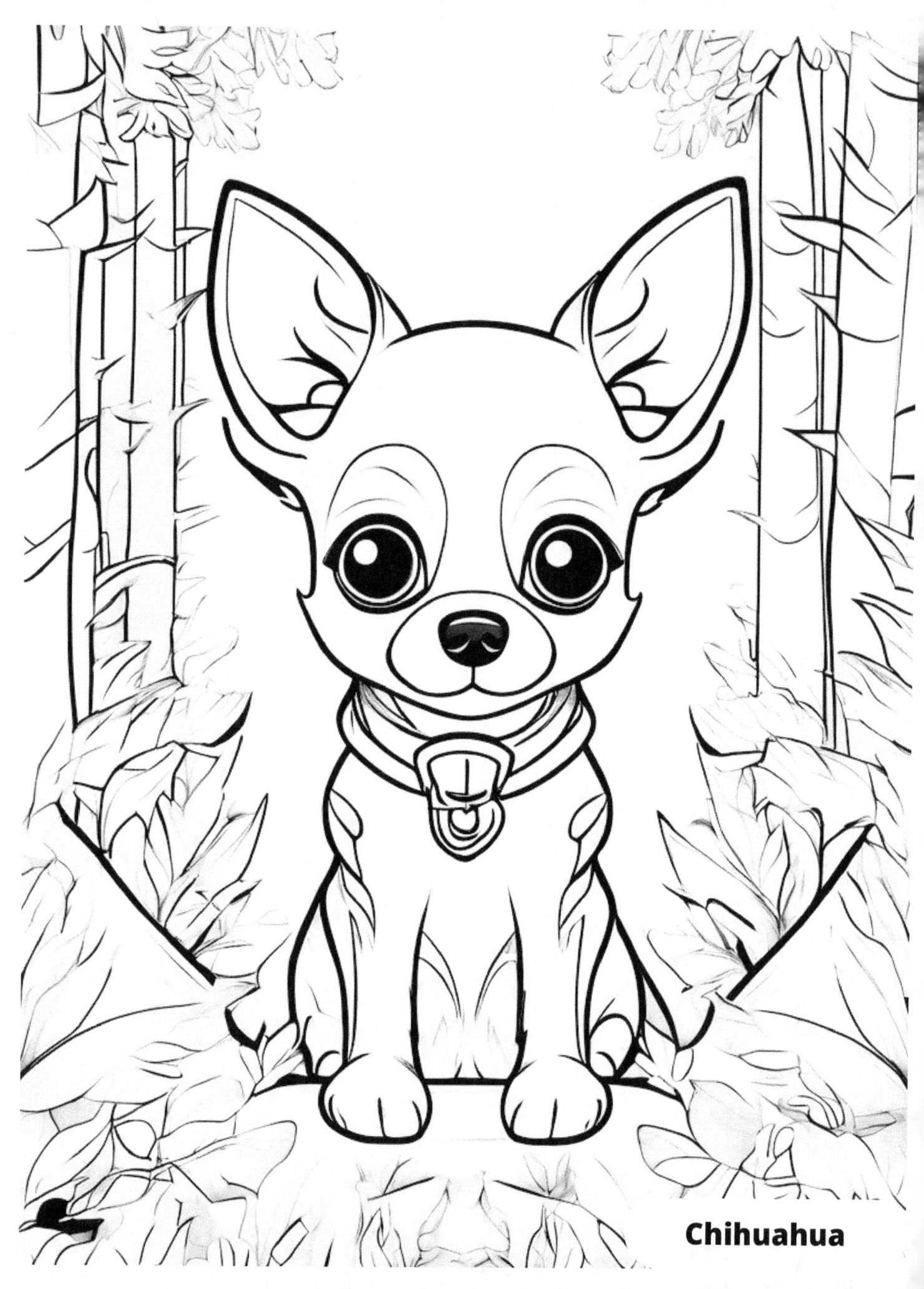

Chihuahua

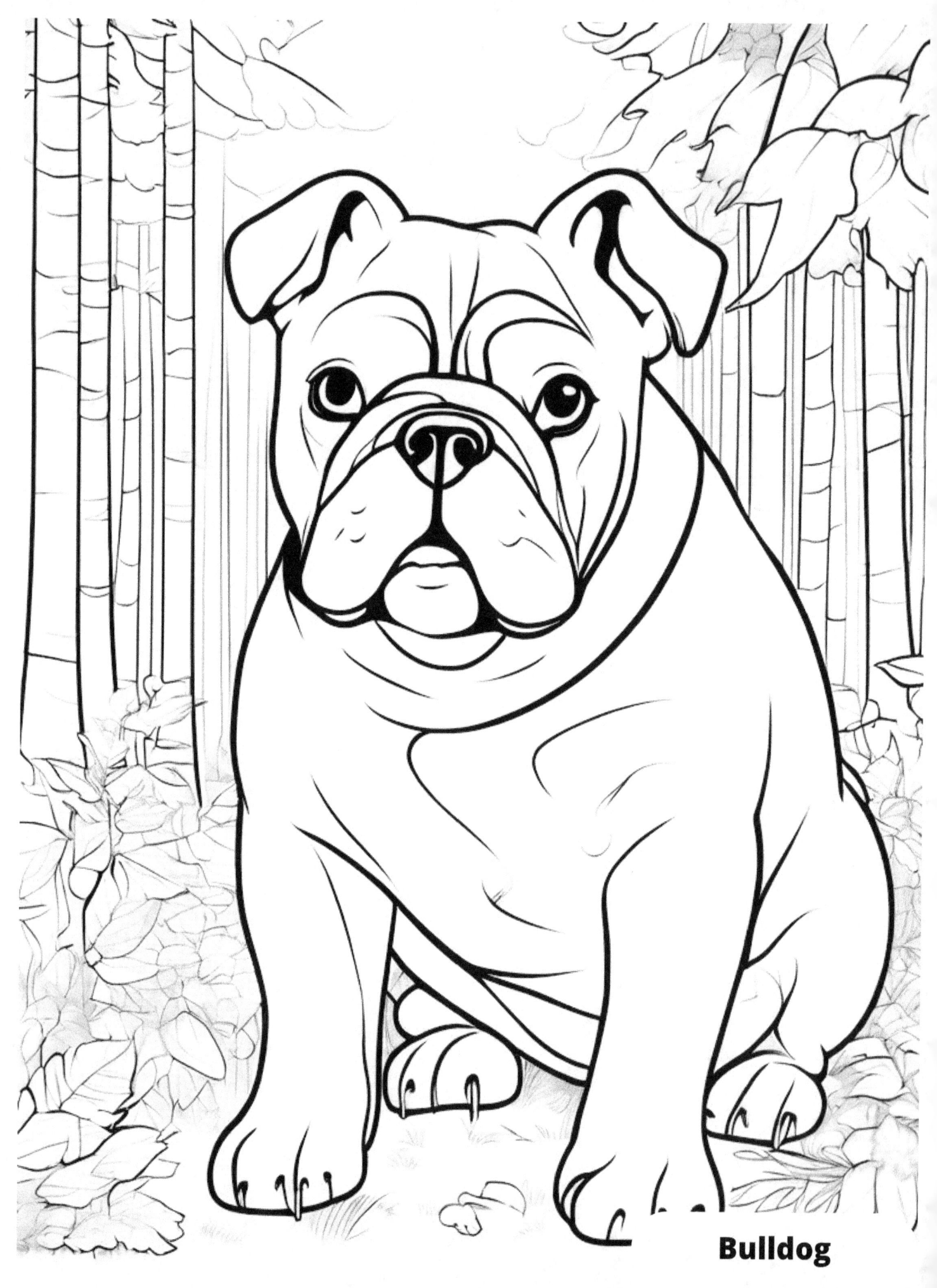

Bulldog

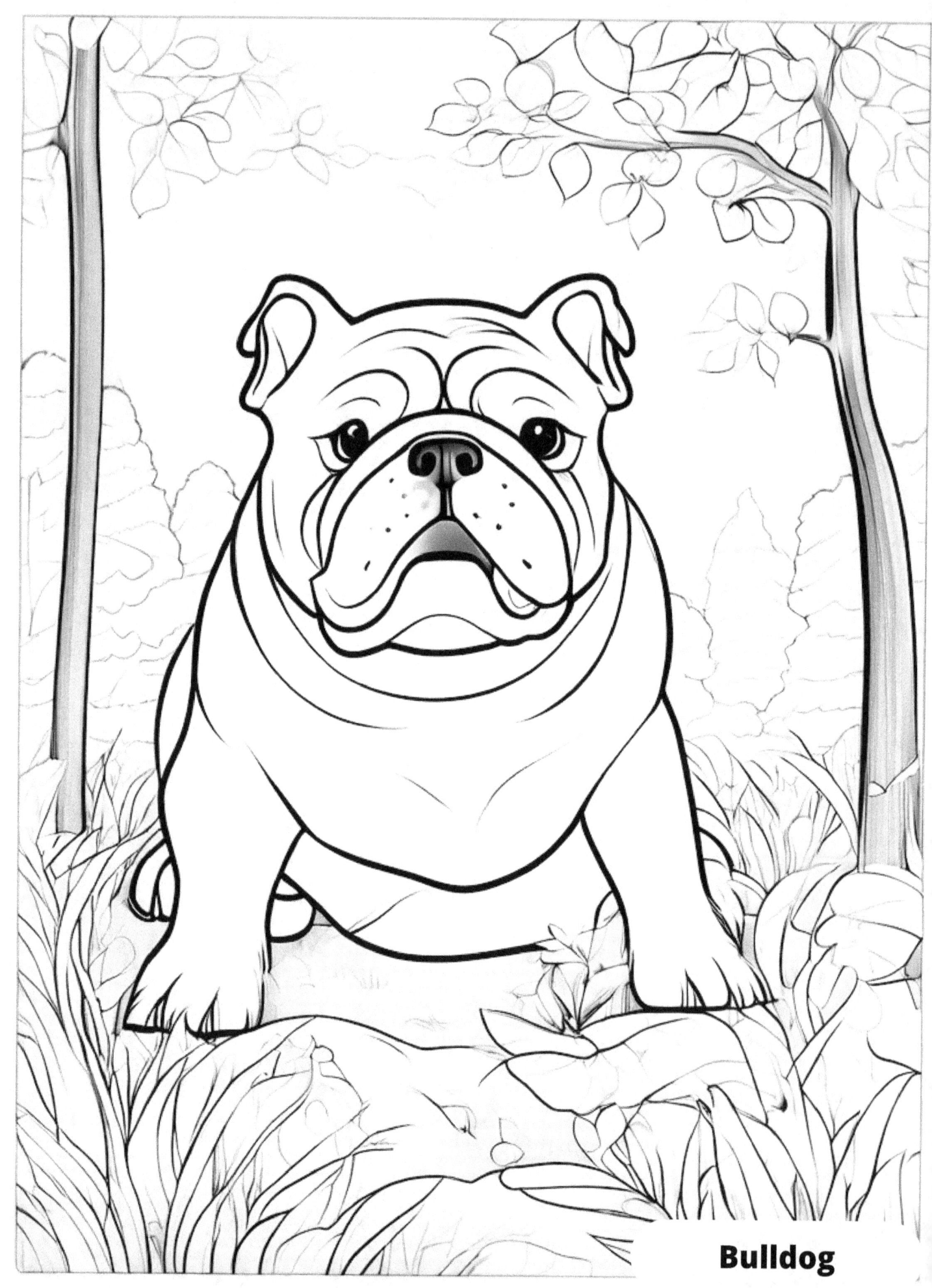

Bulldog

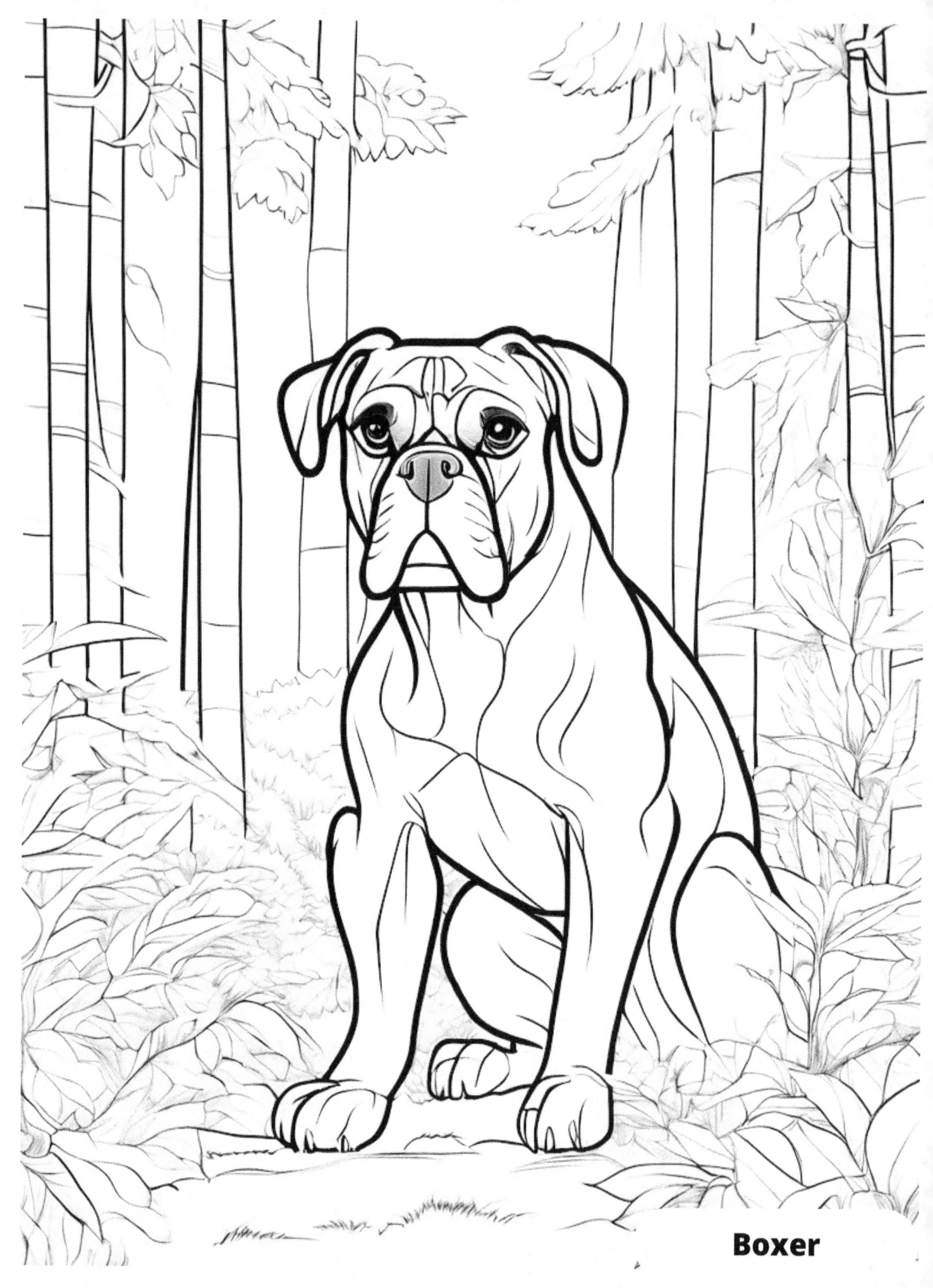

Boxer

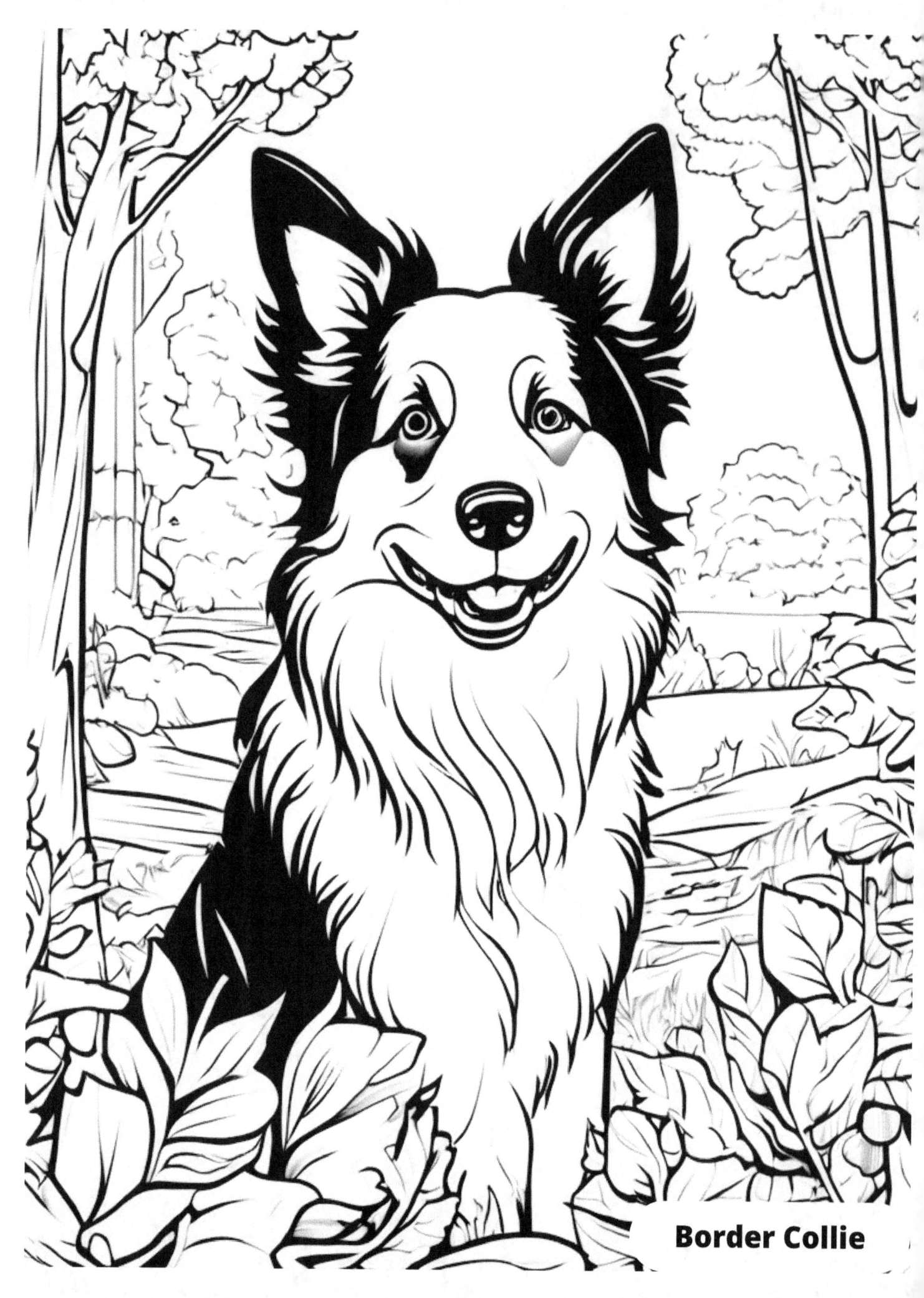

Border Collie

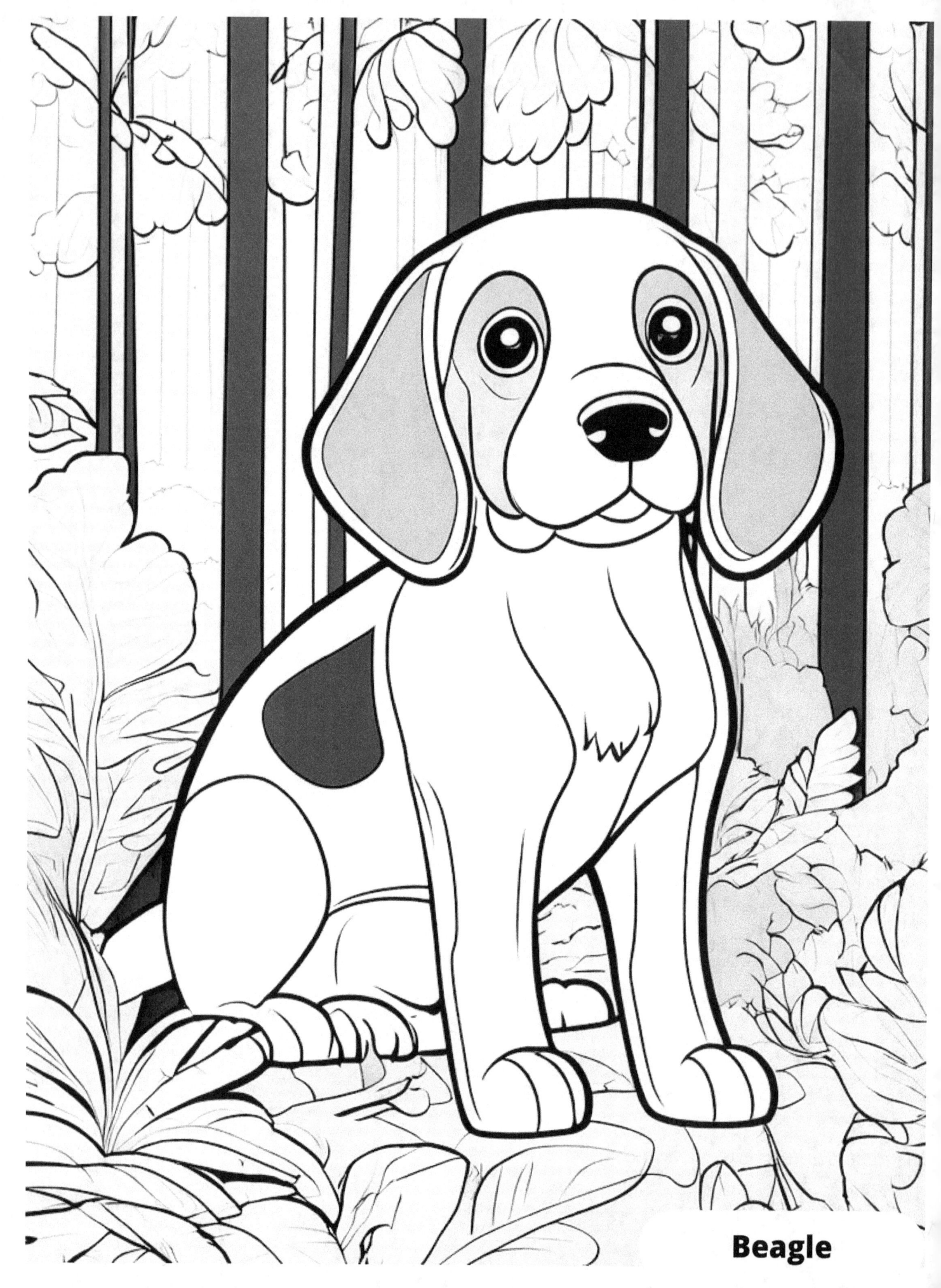

Beagle

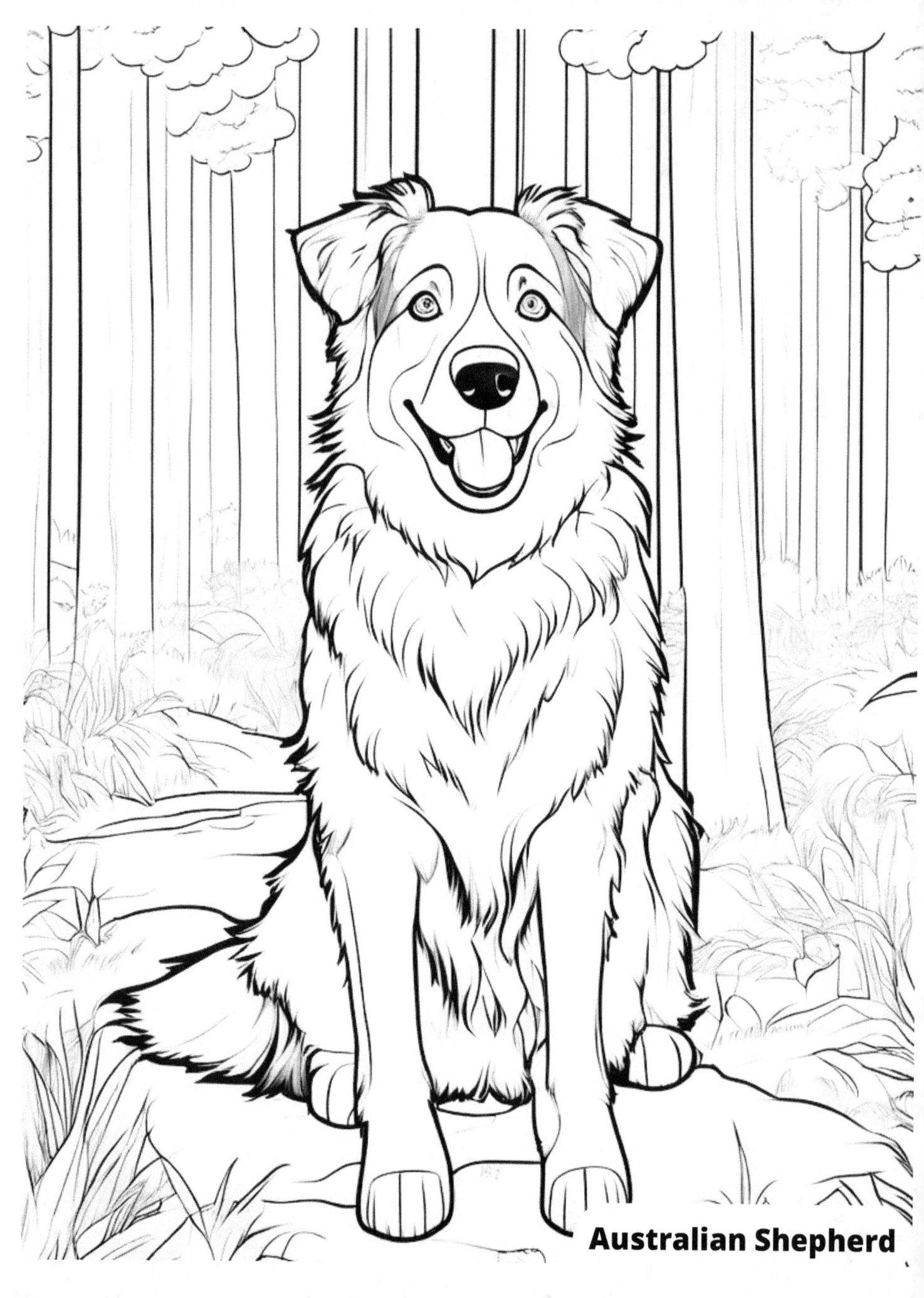

Australian Shepherd

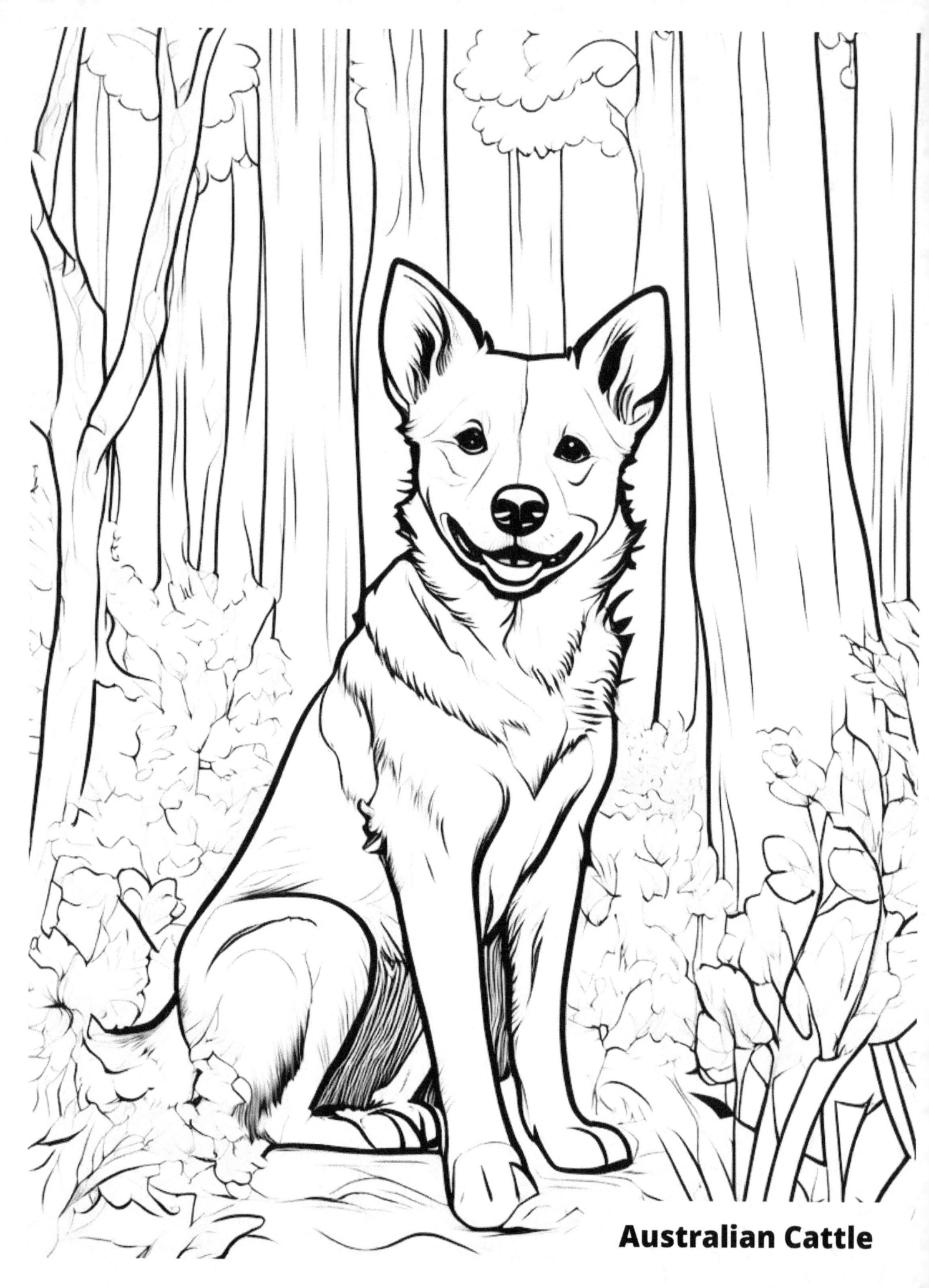

Australian Cattle

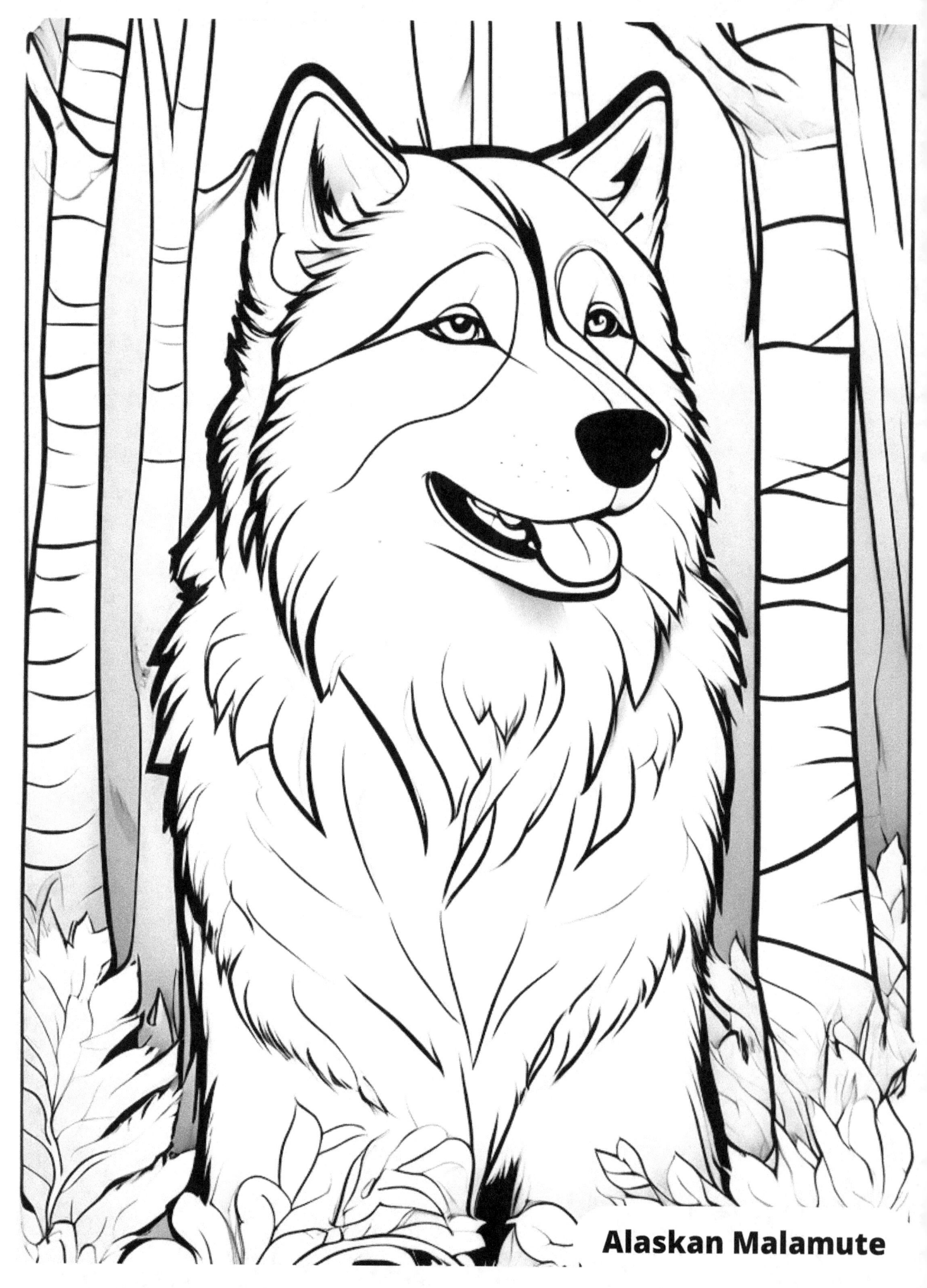

Alaskan Malamute

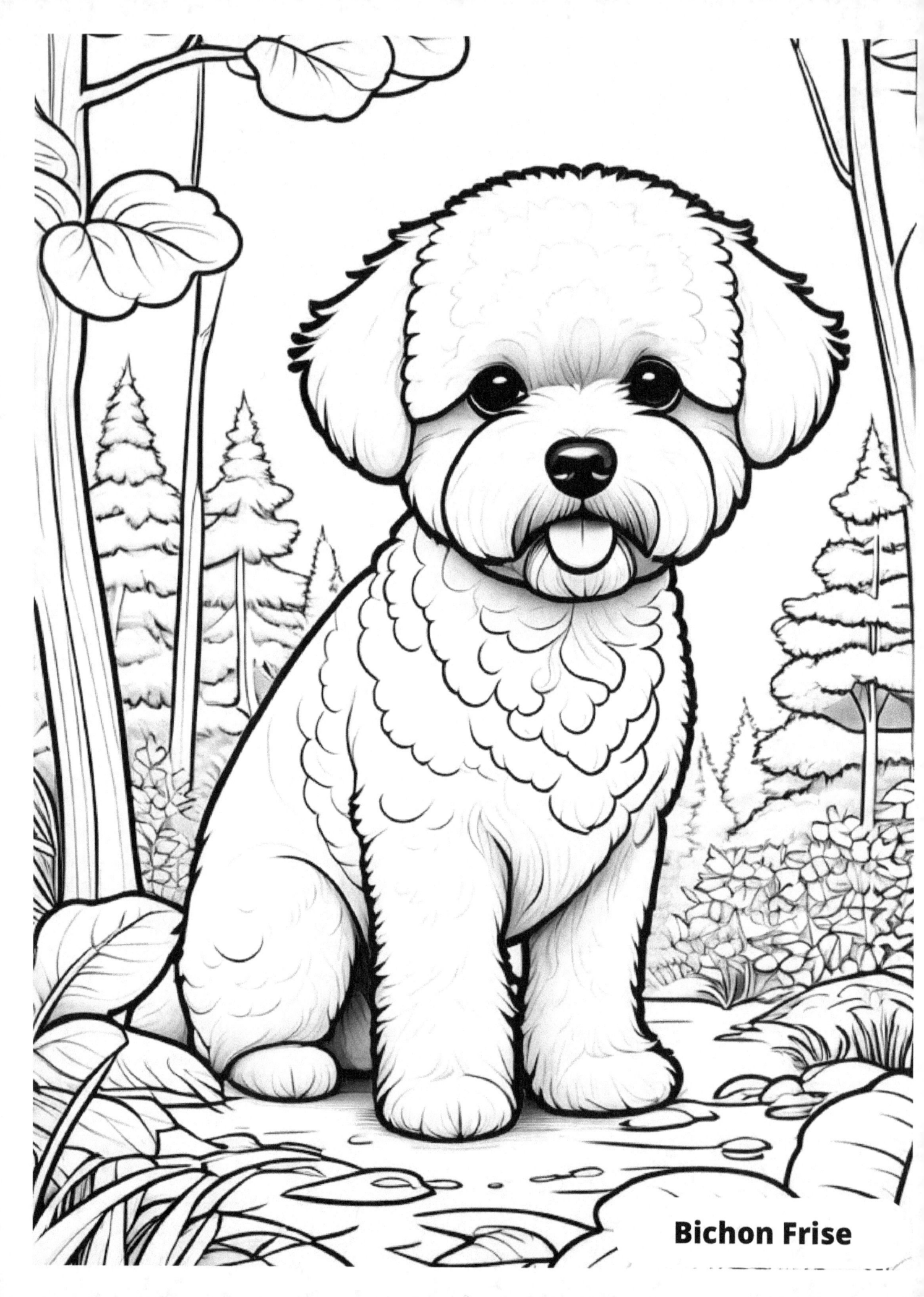

Bichon Frise

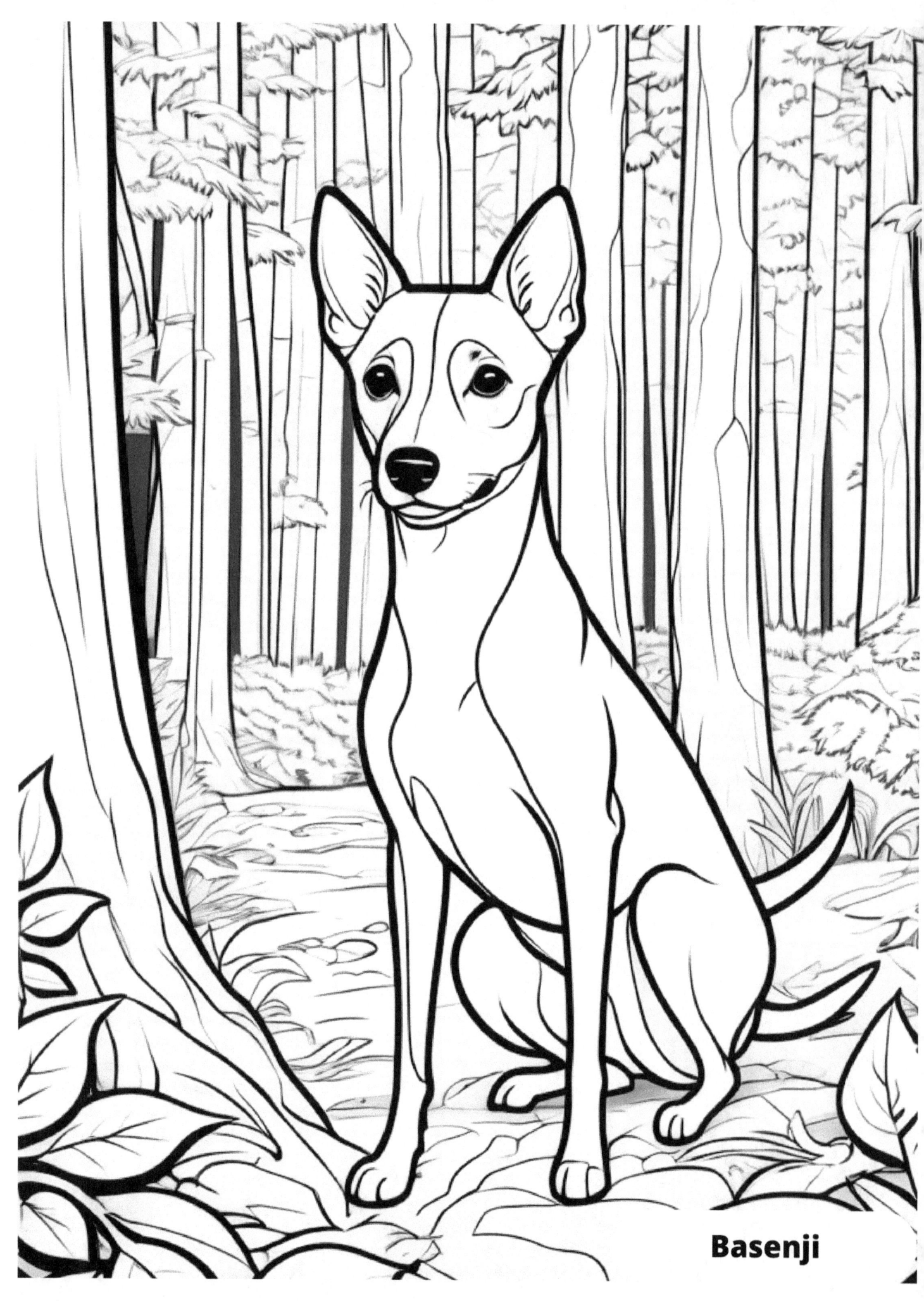

Basenji

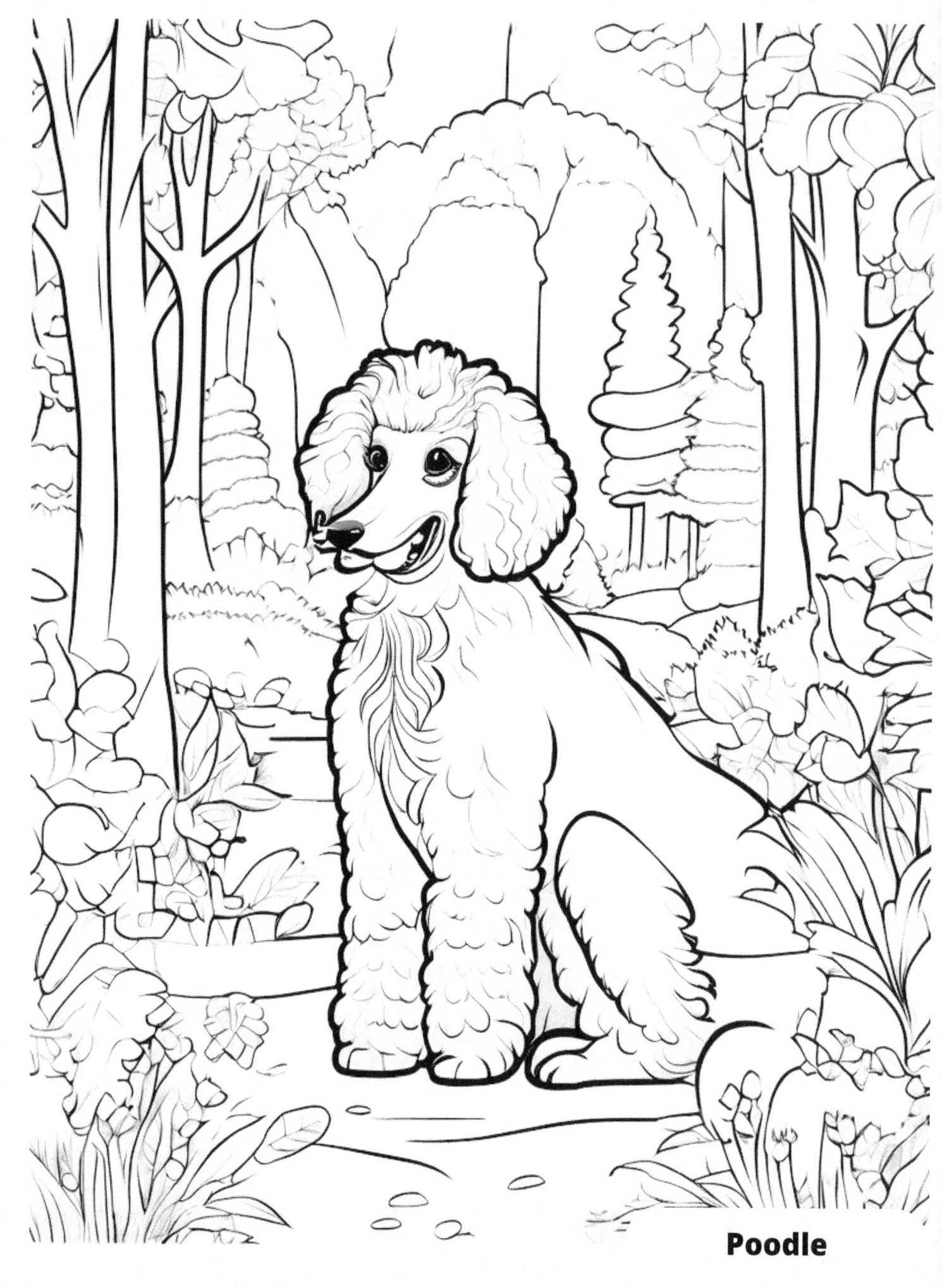

Poodle

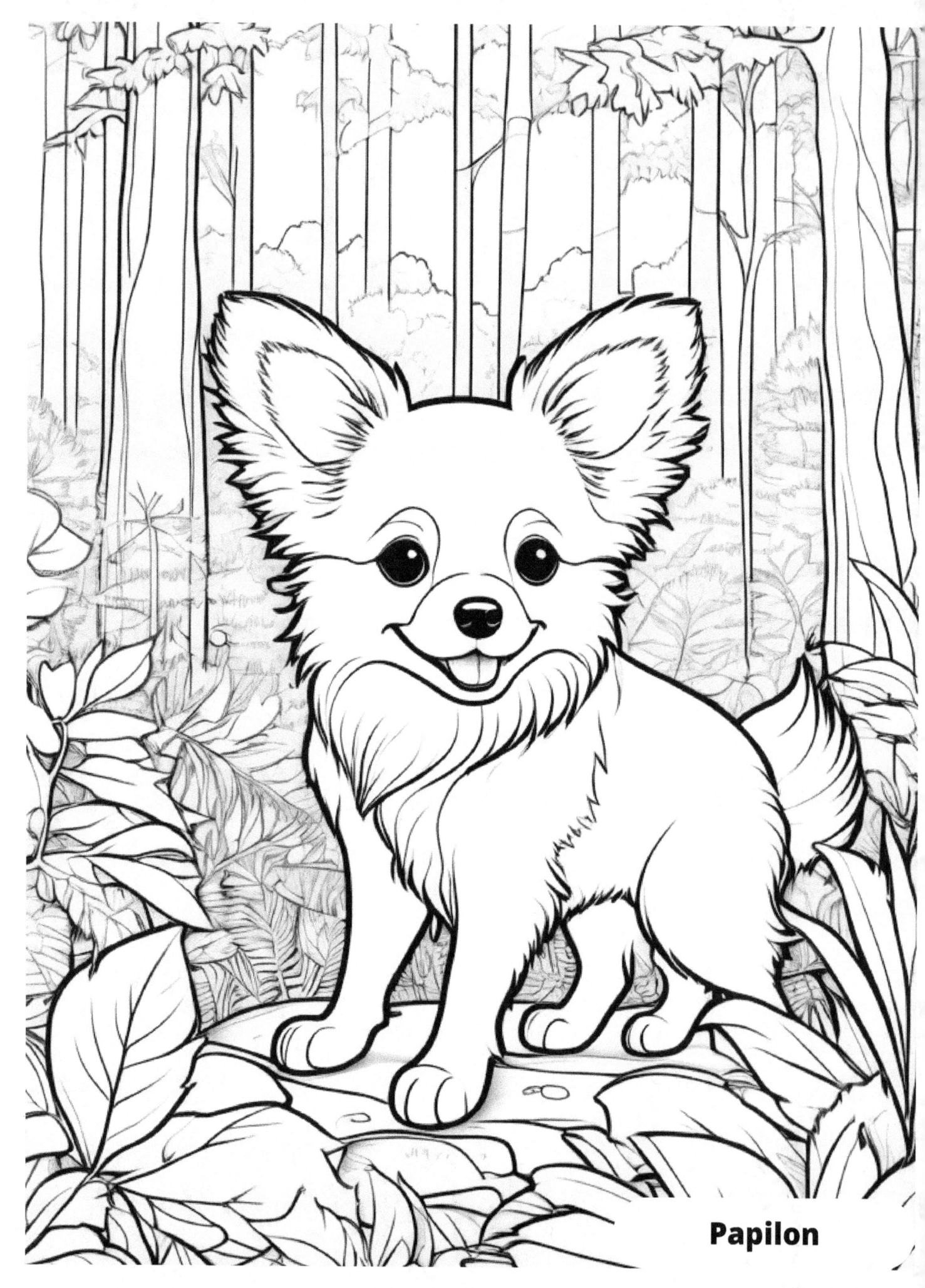

Papilon

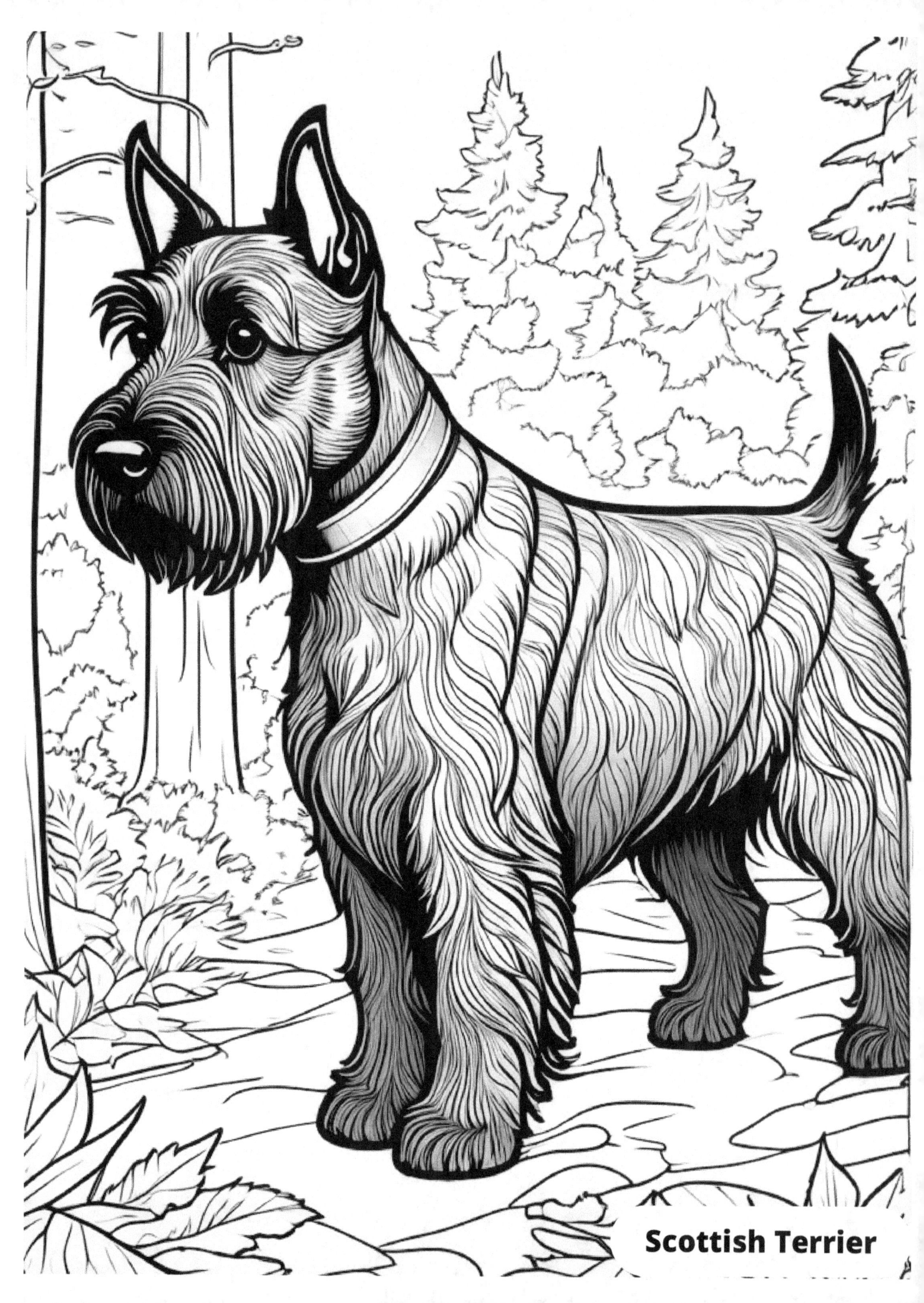

Scottish Terrier

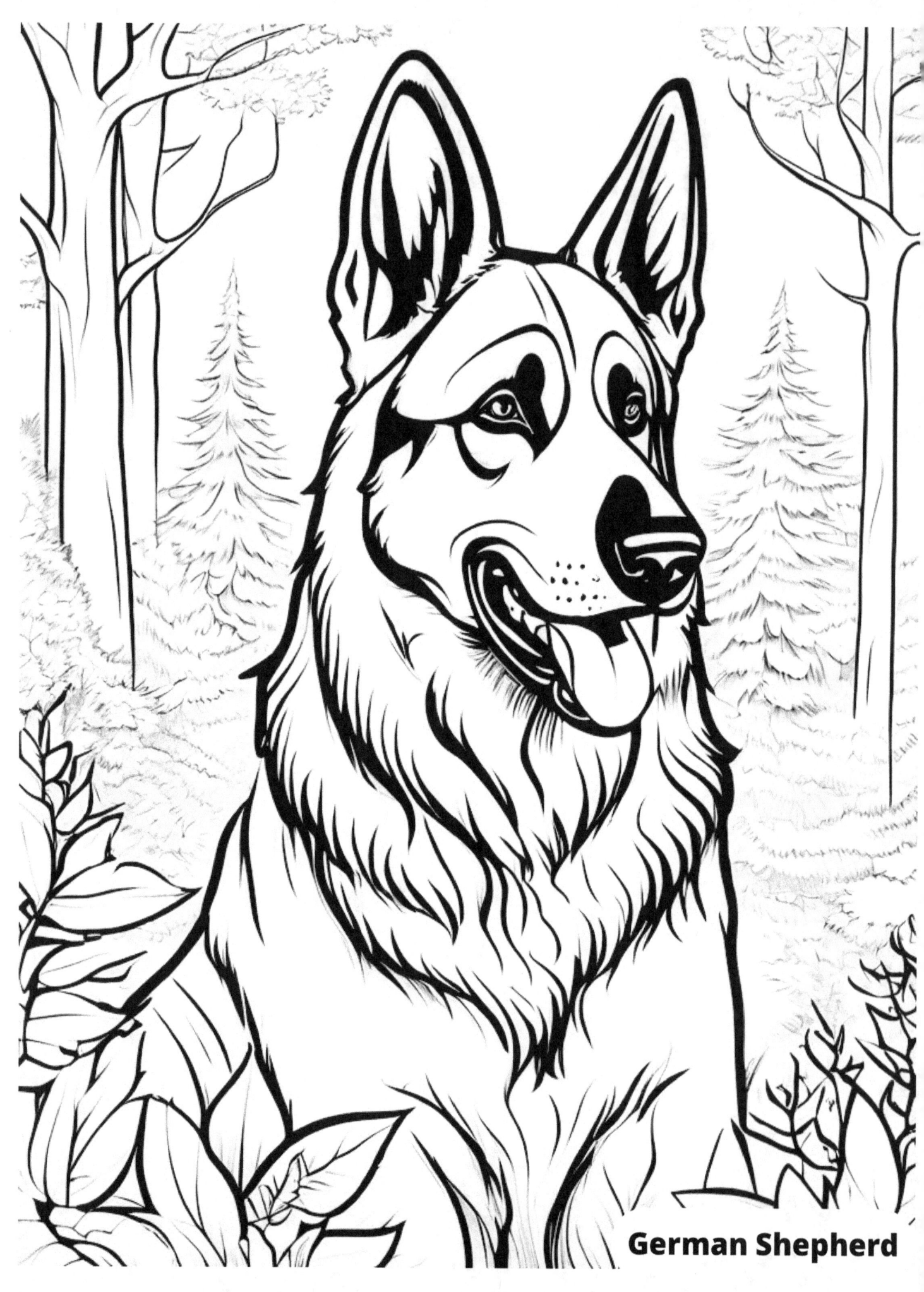

German Shepherd

www.ingramcontent.com/pod-product-compliance
Lightning Source LLC
Chambersburg PA
CBHW081000290526
45795CB00009B/3019